CW00522463

switch

stand out, get the right job
and accelerate your career

PREE SARKAR

RETHINK PRESS

First published in Great Britain in 2020 by
Rethink Press (www.rethinkpress.com)

Cover image © The Switch Method Co Pty Ltd

Praise

'I was introduced to The Switch Method several months back when I was looking to take the next step in my career. At the time my approach was pretty scattergun, I had an idea of where I wanted to be but was unsure how to get there. I learnt that I had to own it, be clear on what I wanted, refine my personal brand, build a list of companies and approach them as if I was prospecting for the biggest sale of my life. The final steps covered how to influence and create leverage through the interview process. After embracing it wholeheartedly, I quickly gathered momentum in my pursuit. I landed four interviews at target companies, three of which made an offer and I am now working in an amazing role that I love. Pree helped me change my job and the trajectory of my career significantly and I'm forever grateful!'

> — **Cameron Perkins,** Account Executive, Falcon.io

'*Switch* sets the tone for the future of work with expert guidance on how to manage your career in this new decade. It is packed with insights, stories, tips and thoughts which will be invaluable for people in flux with their jobs.'

> — **Sharryn Napier,** Vice President & Regional Director ANZ, Qlik

'Pree has a tremendous ability to marry the right candidate, with the right role and the right employer. Translating 10 years of this insight makes this book a compelling read.'

— **Matt Bolton,** Senior Director, Channels and Alliances Ecosystem, ServiceNow

'I wish I had this book to read ten years ago. Pree has outlined a blueprint of what you should do throughout your career, to ensure you are talking the right steps to enable your full potential and possibility for professional growth.'

— **Paul Tuffs,** Director of Commercial Sales, Rackspace

'Wherever you may find yourself on the way to your next career destination, the practical approaches in this book will quickly take you there. The proven strategies and meaningful actions will help you take full advantage moving towards your new, purpose-driven opportunity. The right job is closer than you may think!'

— **Mark Souter,** Director, Human Capital Management for Asia Pacific, Oracle

'In an ever-changing world, trying to get clarity on the next step in your career is more challenging than ever. This book will help all those seeking to understand how to make the best decisions for the future.'

— **Gerry Tucker,** Managing Director ANZ, NICE Systems

'It amazes me that only a small percentage of people know how to effectively seek their next career role. How many in your experience do a good job of building and executing a career plan? *Switch* gives us all an outstanding guideline to achieving your next dream job in a planned and timely manner. I recommend this book as mandatory reading for everybody considering their next career move.'

— **John Smibert,** CEO, Sales Leader Forums and Founder, Sales Masterminds APAC

'If you want to make your next big move and don't know how, it really is simple: follow The Switch Method. *Switch* is by far the most practical book you will read on your career journey. A truly hands-on planning tool to guide you through the steps to landing your next role.'

— **Jacclyn Nautiyal,** Executive Manager, Executive Rewards and Strategy, Suncorp Group

'Pree Sarkar masterfully explains how to future-proof your career and soar in your dream role. We live in the age of automation where the bots are coming for everyone's job, disrupting careers and livelihoods. Markets change, companies struggle to survive and employment has never been less stable. People inevitably change jobs but often go from the frying pan into the fire. *Switch* shows us how to de-risk any career and explains exactly how to thrive by combining value with purpose so that work is both enjoyable and rewarding.

This book is a must read for anyone thinking about changing their career or employer.'

> — **Tony J. Hughes,** Co-Founder, Sales IQ Global, Best Selling Author, Sales Enablement and Keynote Speaker

'*Switch* is packed with experience and authenticity. I feel reinvigorated after reading this.'

> — **Daniel Churches,** National Software Solutions Sales Manager, NTT / Formerly Dimension Data

'*Switch* is a must read for any busy business professional, wanting to build a successful and rewarding career but struggling to know how to do it. Pree Sarkar condenses his 20 years of industry experience into clear and actionable nuggets of wisdom, using war stories, frameworks and imagery to convey complex ideas in a structured and easily accessible way. The future of work may be uncertain, but with Pree Sarkar as your guide, your career path is in safe hands.'

> — **Cian McLoughlin,** CEO Trinity Perspectives, Best Selling Author, Award Winning Blogger, Sales Expert

To Petrina, my best friend, high-school sweetheart, wife and mother of our three children. Your act of courage in the face of fear, to call and ask for that job, is the inspiration behind this book. Your strength, sacrifice and encouragement have enabled me to make it a reality... and it is our gift to share with the world.

Contents

Introduction

There's been a switch over the last thirty years in how people choose and change jobs and build their careers. There's been a change in how companies select, retain and promote employees. The internet, mobile devices and social networking has dramatically disrupted the old practices and made way for the instant, connected and rapidly evolving workplace we are a part of today.

LinkedIn, Glassdoor, applicant tracking systems (ATS) and artificial intelligence (AI) are impacting current and future job changes and how companies hire in a way people do not fully understand yet. It is critical that you **make the switch** to thriving in a digital, social and connected age of work and career management.

My goal in writing this book is to help you pursue and get the right job for your next career move so that you are happy, well rewarded, successful and making an impact in your workplace and community. And furthermore, future proof your career by using The Switch Method as your operating system to get the jobs you want, plan a career path and live the life you desire.

No one teaches how to get the right job or manage a career over a lifetime at school or work (and they still don't). In fact, people didn't used to talk about changing jobs openly at all. It was seen as disloyal to their current employer and made people feel insecure, and it can still be frowned upon.

Some of you will have parents who worked with the same organisation for ten to twenty-five years or more (mine certainly did). You may even have done so yourself. The beliefs, values and behaviours you inherited in your formative career years shaped the beliefs, values and behaviours you currently hold about work, careers and changing jobs.

Career principles in the baby-boomer generation (born 1946–1963) looked something like this:

1. Get a good education

2. Get a good job with a reputable employer

3. Get trained, developed and promoted to your highest potential

4. Retire

The problem is that what worked in the past **does not work now.** The seven new principles for career acceleration are:

1. Loyalty is dead and performance is king. You are only as good as your results. Results are more important than your tenure in the company; they determine whether you will get promoted, remain where you are or be made redundant. When the mutual value proposition (MVP) between employer and you as an employee no longer exists, it's time for them to find someone else and for you to move on.

2. Culture and fit are more important than brand name and strategy. You are likely to choose to stay with an employer based on the culture and potential to succeed in the current job on offer rather than on the name on the door and prospects for long-term progression.

3. Your skills are for hire and you are the CEO of your company of one. Your employment is a one-client contract with an unclear end date. Employers are becoming clients, and you as an employee fulfil the roles of the specialist service provider. The team is a task force, and when the mission is complete, the team is disbanded.

4. You need to maximise your value to your employer. You are responsible for your learning, development and career path. This is not the

responsibility of your boss or employer. If something can be done faster, better or at a lower cost, you are at risk of being replaced. Companies will continue to look for the best value for money. The offshore production model is mature, AI and bots are emerging and beginning to replace people in jobs that can be automated.

5. Learn to work in your job and on your career every day. My experience shows that people typically have eight to ten jobs between the ages of twenty to forty-five, so at any given point in time, you are thirty to thirty-six months away from a job change. Always be prepared for that change.

6. Master how to market yourself to employers. Being able to promote yourself to secure your next job (whether internally or externally) while working in your current one is a critical skill that you need to master to survive and thrive in a business environment that is constantly changing.

7. Your network is your net worth and referrals are rocket fuel. You will shoot to the top of an interview shortlist with a strong referral as well as internal supporters. People are online, socially connected and instantly accessible 24/7. If you aren't prominent socially, you do not exist in people's current memory. Good personal branding and social capital will increase

your influence, resulting in inbound career opportunities and accelerating your career.

Some people are earning $500,000 per annum by the age of forty-five, while others are lucky to get to $200,000 by the time they retire. So, what is the secret of the lucky ones' success?

That secret is what we will cover throughout the course of this book. The Switch Method is a roadmap and a process that combines success principles from thousands of the lucky ones into an easy-to-follow step-by-step process. So without further ado, let's get started with an overview of this invaluable method.

How To Read This Book

This book has been organised into four steps, with three key factors that contribute to success at each step. If you want to improve any given step or a factor within a step, go to that chapter in the book and you will have the information you need to solve your problem. The Switch Method is designed to be a constant companion and a step-by-step guide from the moment you think about changing jobs right through to the time you accept the offer letter for the job you desire. Keep coming back to this book every time you encounter an obstacle in your quest for the right job for you.

I hate Mondays	⟶	read Ownership
I'm not sure what the right job is for me	⟶	read Clarity
I'm not making the time to look for a new job	⟶	read Focus
I'm not comfortable promoting myself	⟶	read Value
I don't have good career marketing materials	⟶	read Build
I don't have social presence	⟶	read Engage
I'm not sure if it's the right time to move	⟶	read Timing
I don't know who I want to work for	⟶	read Research
I'm not getting the right interviews	⟶	read Connect
I'm not succeeding at interviews	⟶	read Interview
I'm not hearing back from employers after interviews	⟶	read Follow-up
I'm not getting the offers I want	⟶	read Negotiate

SECTION ONE
INTRODUCING THE
SWITCH METHOD

ONE

The Birth Of The Switch Method

Problems in the workplace

We go in to work to do the best we can with the resources available to us. We want to succeed, be happy, be rewarded and make a difference. Yet many of us experience the reality of problems, which are often beyond our control. These include:

- Being overworked and suffering stress due to short deadlines, high expectations and chronic under-staffing

- Being under-paid compared to colleagues within and outside the organisation

- Having to travel excessively for work and lacking quality time with family, which can impact relationships at home

- A lack of growth opportunities internally, as well as lack of recognition of potential for growth – we're doing a job well, so we are kept there as long as possible

- A lack of ability to make changes

- A lack of support from your manager

- Our own lack of belief in the product or service provided by the company

- Our lack of belief in the senior management team and future direction of the company

If you do decide to look for a new job, you will need to confront a new set of challenges:

- There are fewer and fewer mid to senior professional and management roles as you move up in the organisation, and the number of candidates wanting these roles number more than the positions available

- You need the time to update your resume, apply for new jobs and talk to prospective employers

- Communicating your value/contribution in a few sentences, knowing that recruiters will skim over your resume rather than read right through it, and potentially provide an inaccurate response based on an inadequate review of your resume

- Identifying early on whether the role and the company are the right fit for you

- Not getting the right interviews nor the opportunity to have a discussion around your suitability for a role

- A lengthy recruitment process which comes to nothing after numerous interviews

- A lack of understanding of how you rank compared to other applicants

- Feeling pigeon-holed into a role or industry and not being allowed to change lanes

- Being over-qualified or under-qualified

- Interviewing for a role which is a level below your current or previous job

- Gaining understanding of and support for the value of your transferrable skills

- Ageism and being on the wrong side of the average age for a job/level

- Lack of follow up from recruiters after interviews

When you're faced with problems and challenges such as these, it is easy to feel trapped or stuck in a job and forced to wait for the 'right' job to present itself.

Let's face it, life's not fair. Work's not fair. Income and opportunity are not given equally. Some people seem to have all the luck in the world. They get promotions, they are seen at the right places with the right people and get incredible career breaks. If they get made redundant, they find a better job well before they've spent the redundancy payout. If they change jobs, they manage to get great roles. They seem happy, well appreciated, earn good money and have work-life balance. They out-grow roles and out-earn peers faster than most of us.

So, what is the secret of their success?

My first job

Throughout high school and university, I struggled with a lack of direction and felt average. I didn't stand out in anything and nothing stood out to me. I had no idea what I wanted to do when I grew up. My family had an enviable line up of men and women who had achieved notable professional success in a variety of fields, but rather than inspiring me, at the time, they seemed superhuman, legendary and unreachable. No one and nothing seemed to be interesting enough to pursue.

In the late 90s, after completing a Post Graduate Diploma in Management, my peers and I had campus interviews. Ogilvy & Mather, GE and other notable companies like GE, Xerox, Foote Cone and Belding were hiring.

I applied, along with thirty-five other hopeful graduates, to Xerox, and much to my surprise, I was the only one who was selected and offered the job that year.

At first, I felt euphoric about starting on my new career journey. But once the life of a trainee sales account executive became reality, I found it soul-destroying. I was door-knocking companies in industrial and business parks to generate interest in photocopiers. Ask, get rejected; ask, get rejected; ask, get the door slammed (mostly metaphorically and a few times literally).

The only predictable thing in my job was rejection, office by office, hour by hour. Had someone told me at the victorious moment of being offered the job that this was what my life would become, I would rather have stuck a pin in my eye. I felt trapped and increasingly frustrated. A former classmate now at GE was planning to travel to twelve countries in twelve months as part of his orientation in his new role, while I was going to be travelling on foot around the depressing wastelands of commercial and industrial estates.

A roadmap to success

This difficult period lasted for months until I got invited to go to sales process training offsite. I was excited for two reasons. First, I would have a break from prospecting for business and facing more rejection. Second, I would go to a resort, get fed all day, and just sit and listen to someone talk. Easy! It beat getting my feet on the street.

What I didn't expect was how learning a sales process would change my life. For the first time, someone taught me a step-by-step method covering how to choose the right target customers, introduce myself, ask for the opportunity, discover needs, present a compelling solution, handle objections, negotiate and reach agreement to close the sale. I was given the roadmap for success and the skills to move from feeling rejected and unsuccessful to winning new business and achieving my goals.

I left that training session with clarity, the confidence to ask once more and a burning desire to succeed. With a clear process to follow, I knew how to navigate every situation. Immediately, I noticed a difference. I had more sales and fewer rejections. Within a few months, I started achieving my targets, and within six months, I won my first sales contest by reaching 130% of my targets. I was rewarded with an all-expenses-paid trip with other qualifiers to Madrid, Spain.

And then, I exceeded targets for the next six quarters leading up to a President's Club award for exceptional performance the following year. I had the respect of my managers and my peers, and I experienced that sweet moment when I realised I was earning more than my parents' combined income. They couldn't believe it, and nor could I. At twenty-four, I had achieved a significant, tangible result for the first time in my life, and that had been acknowledged by everyone who mattered to me in my professional and personal world.

I had made the switch from feeling average to accomplished in my first professional job.

With a reliable roadmap in my hands and skills for the journey, I could succeed in anything. And I had two years of results and rewards to prove it. I also saw myself differently. Some much-needed self-respect and confidence had appeared alongside the success. This gave me the clarity to recognise what I was good at, loved to do and got paid well for – engaging people, discovering their needs, solving their problems, advising them and getting them to take action. My personal transformation and success at this early stage developed into a belief and passion for training and personal development.

Learning how to ask for the job

After three years in the job, I felt like I was stagnating. It was time to move on and learn new skills. But I didn't know how to go about finding the 'right' next job for me. I felt stuck and the frustration started to grow again.

My wife – girlfriend back then – had finished a course in interior design and was doing an internship at a company that imported exotic carpets and furnishings. Her boss asked her to check his rolodex and cull the business cards he no longer needed. As she looked through them, she came across the card of the editor of a leading interior design magazine.

For a few years, she had been dreaming of what it would be like to work for that magazine. Her heart began to race and excitement rose as she had a crazy idea to call the editor and ask for a job. At the same time, nausea and fear crept up on her. This was totally outside her comfort zone, but she dialled the phone number anyway.

'Hi, my name is Petrina,' she said. 'I love your magazine, and if you have any jobs available, I would love to work for you.'

At first there was silence, and then a short conversation progressed. Finally, the editor said, 'Can you meet me on Tuesday at 11am?' And yes, she got the job. Over the next ten years, she went on to build her career with industry-leading companies by reaching out and proactively asking for jobs she wanted, over and over again.

Petrina made the switch. She overcome her fear of rejection and the tension within her. Her courage and boldness inspired me. I learned for the first time that when you contact the hiring manager and ask for the job you want, you might actually get it! This beats the usual 'apply, apply, no reply' routine that I was going through. It was far better to step out of the queue and get one-on-one.

'Ask and it will be given to you; seek and you will find; knock and the door will be opened to you. For everyone who asks receives; the one who seeks finds; and to the one who knocks, the door will be opened.'

— Matthew, Chapter 7, verses 7–8.
The Holy Bible, New International Version

A change of direction

I reached out to a targeted employer to secure my second job in 2002, and then reached out again in 2005, and again (internally) in 2007. I knew what I wanted, positioned myself favourably, targeted the right people and influenced my way into a great role. Each job change was an intentional step up towards my career goals. Each switch required a change in mindset and each success made my belief in asking stronger.

At thirty-one, I became one of the youngest sales directors for FedEx Office. The managers who reported to me, as well as a good number of their direct reports, were much older than I was. I led three managers and eighteen direct reports, turning around demotivated, under-performing employees to create a winning team, and was instrumental in setting the business unit up for the best results it had had in years. I had my dream job, a high-performance sales team and a great leadership team. And then, on the eve of the 2008 global financial crisis, the company made 220 people redundant and quietly closed my business unit.

It was devastating. A team that had become a family at work was disbanded. And my family at home, with two kids under six and a new mortgage, had *no income*. Stuck again, I was frustrated and fearful as I had not been in this situation before – unemployed and responsible for a family. Like many, my wife and I had agreed that we would start a family and one of us would stay at home for the kids, so she had given up her job and career. It was humbling to write to the bank to say we were facing financial hardship and needed a mortgage holiday. I asked for six months, the bank gave me four months. The pressure was high, and we needed income soon.

I was asked by the managing director of a company to work with their leadership team, transform the sales team and culture as a consultant. This was an eye-opening experience. I discovered first-hand how hard it is for an employer to find the right employees, and vice versa. I also learned, this time as an outsider, how critical the employer and employee MVP is when it comes to determining success and longevity for both. This was a problem I wanted to solve, so I started a recruitment company in late 2008. **It was a switch in role, career and industry.**

Figuring out a process to solve career and talent problems

Wanting to match talented people with great companies, I required processes to secure the right candidates on one hand, as well as secure clients on the other, clients on the one hand, mid-senior candidates on the other hand. These are not job seekers; they are typically people who are happy, well appreciated, performing well, but could be tempted to consider their next move. I had to figure out how to get them to switch from good to great, so I developed a method to engage passive candidates and help them connect with hiring managers who wanted to build high-performance teams.

I became an advisor to hiring managers, consulting with them about culture and fit, talent attraction strategy, employer branding and hiring best practices. At the same time, I became an advisor to mid-senior professionals and managers, coaching them about career strategy, personal branding, interview skills and job selection. I have done this across Fortune 500 publicly traded companies, startups and fast-growing companies over the last 10 years.

I am now fortunate enough to have reached a point in my life where I have been rated by LinkedIn as a top 1% recruiter and have been recognised by presitigious bodies in the recruitment industry.

I believe that the best opportunities and experiences lie on the other side of what may seem like insurmountable obstacles at the time. A series of switch moments in which we change our mindset, learn new things and take action in the face of doubt, fear and prior failure allows us to cross the gap into a new level of work and life.

Feeling average and directionless is now a distant memory. I love what I do, am good at it, well rewarded and make a difference in the world. Everything in my life has led to this point of time. I have used my professional experience with thousands of executives and managers, and my own experience too, to create a reliable process to get the right job as well as a set of career management skills. It's all called **The Switch Method**, and you can follow this step-by-step process to find the jobs you want and build a career you can look back on in celebration with a deep sense of satisfaction, meaning and purpose.

TWO

The Theory Of The Switch Method

PRINCIPLE

Switch from confusion to a high-definition vision of your future.

You are likely to be reading this book because you are looking for something that's missing right now in your current job or the most recent job you've had. You may have already achieved a degree of success over the last ten to twenty years and circumstances have made you to decide to change jobs.

Changing jobs is stressful and challenging – you could experience more highs and lows than a roller-coaster ride before you land the next job. But what if I told you that you could have what you want by applying the core principles and utilising the practical tools in this book? By embracing these concepts for the future, you could build a great career made up of a succession of right jobs.

Would you like to have:

- Total clarity and focus on the right fit for you?

- A high profile in your industry where your insights and experience are sought after?

- Strong relevance and relationships with the people and companies that matter to you?

- The ability to maximise your influence to get the job you want?

The Switch Method will show you how.

The Switch Method is based on real-world failure and success that's taking place right now in people's careers. I have seen it day-in and day-out. This model is the result of years of observation, learning, analysis and application, and is underpinned by my experience of:

1. More than fifteen years in a corporate career as a hiring manager and an individual contributor

2. More than ten years as an executive recruiter and career advisor

3. Over 20,000 hours of experience at the convergence of client and candidate conversations

4. Over 10,000 interviews with career professionals and managers

5. Over 5,000 post-interview debriefs with hiring managers and candidates

6. Thousands of job briefs from global companies

The Switch Method is a job change and career management process that will remove the frustrations and challenges you are likely to face in finding the right job. You will feel more in control, confident, clear-headed and happy. This method is an essential roadmap to keep in front of you through the exploratory journey of changing jobs and considering new career opportunities as it provides a pathway to accelerate your career to your desired destination.

Before I outline the four steps of The Switch Method, let's first consider where you find yourself today on the roadmap of your job and career journey.

The story of constant change in the workplace

More than ever before, the forces of change at work are evolving rapidly. If we reflect on the changes in the workplace, we will see they generally revolve around three metaphorical destinations. For the sake of illustration, I have called these *New Town, Mount Pleasant* and *Problem Vale,* and as the names suggest, each one has distinct situations, challenges and opportunities.

These will be cyclical throughout your work life as the forces of change impact on your job and career, but there are always exceptions to the rule.

Let's jump in and see at which location you find yourself today.

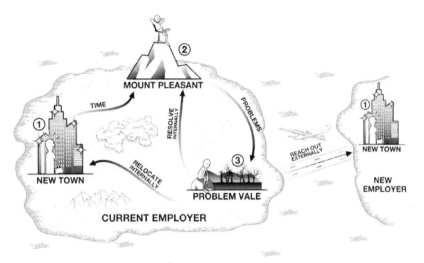

The story of constant change in the workplace

New Town

'It's exciting and there is much to learn,' you would be likely to say in your first month in a new job. Everything is interesting and unknown. It is like the initial few hours outside your hotel room in a town you are visiting for the first time. So many places to go, so many things to see and learn, people to meet, cafés to visit, new streets to walk down and options to explore.

26

You're shown your workspace, the new laptop, perhaps you're given a t-shirt and a notebook and pen with the company logo on it. There are the new faces of those who will work around you – some smiling, some preoccupied, others looking slightly awkward.

As the days go by, you discover the characters. You begin to figure out how things work at this destination and perhaps even have a drink after work with your colleagues. It's all interesting. This new place is great, much like a new pair of shoes you love wearing, or that new song that's everywhere, or the aroma of coffee in the building that is really growing on you. You are working out who are your confidants, your comrades and the ones to be careful of. This is the land of the honeymoon. Enjoy it while it lasts, because things will change.

Mount Pleasant

'I love it here! I'm in the zone,' is what you're likely to say when you settle into your job and things are going well. Everyone is friendly. The job is like your favourite winter jacket, the most comfortable couch or your usual place at a restaurant you like to visit. The coffee on Mount Pleasant is like your oldest and most trustworthy friend and the music is classic, never going out of style.

You like what you do. The job pays well, you are achieving goals, the team around you is great. You are good at the work and have a sense of purpose in your job. The offsite team meetings are fun, people are familiar and reliable, you are making a difference and are getting noticed for it.

Your colleagues like you and you have opportunities to mentor a few of the people around you. Your opinion matters and you are a leader in your peer group. Your manager has acknowledged your efforts and even mentioned the scope for growth and promotion in due time. This is the land of the great marriage. May it never end. Enjoy every day as long as you possibly can, because again, things will change!

Problem Vale

'I feel stuck. Something is different. It's not the company I joined,' you are likely to say when things have changed for the worse and have been that way for a while. It's like the furniture feels old, dusty and needs attention. The fan squeaks and the people are getting on your nerves. You notice that the restaurants in Problem Vale have changed as well – the food is boring and the coffee doesn't do it any more for you. The music makes you want to cringe – the one-hit wonder that is no longer enjoyable.

Things were going well, but then maybe your manager changed. Or one of your best friends at work left for another job, and a new team member started polarising the team. It's just not the same as it used to be. You've found out that the customers are unhappy with the company, which is facing financial pressure and there is talk of a re-organisation. You have noticed instances of bullying or sexual harassment or a 'boys' club'. There's ambiguity in direction and promises have been broken or delayed for three to six months. The work is no longer challenging and you don't feel connected to the big picture anymore. Your life seems to be on hold.

The four choices

You are the author of your story. What are you going to do? You can live with the effect of other people's decisions or you can decide that you will take control of your work (and life too). Should you stay or should you go? I believe that you have four choices.

Choice #1: Watch and wait

You could stay with your current employer in Problem Vale and see if things will change. You might call an old colleague and talk about the 'good old days' at Mount Pleasant, finishing with agreements like 'we must get together soon'. You might envy the energy and enthusiasm in their voice when they talk about their New Town.

The problem is that more often than not, things get worse in Problem Vale. The air is disempowering and takes a toll on your thoughts, beliefs and motivation over a period of time. People who have stayed there for too long find it difficult to leave. They can't go back to Mount Pleasant, they don't like Problem Vale and they don't know the way to New Town, or are afraid to start over again. Most people do what they have always done: they wait until they get laid off, managed out or the situation gets unbearable and they quit.

Choice #2: Resolve the problem

You could go back to Mount Pleasant with your current employer. Take ownership of driving change. Raise the issue with your manager. Ask for more money, ask for more support staff to be hired, agree on more suitable working hours or realign on expectations. Resolve any issues you may have with toxic or polarising colleagues. You may take on new responsibilities. You could take on the challenge of being the champion for change in the areas that concern and impact you the most. If you can initiate true and lasting change, you will be able to head back to *Mount Pleasant.*

Choice #3: Relocate within the organisation

You could return to New Town with your current employer, by moving into a new job internally. Again, take ownership of driving change and raise the issues you have with your manager. Tell them why you need the change, remind them what you have already achieved for them (people have a short memory) and how you are intending to move within the organisation. Ask them to support you as you explore other opportunities – you will need the support of your existing manager to move jobs internally. Get the support of your senior manager (your boss's boss) too; he or she could be an enabler (or an obstacle) down the road.

In essence, get your house in order to move to a new role internally. Speak with human resources (HR) as well as the managers who will potentially oversee the roles you want to work in. Don't wait for an internal announcement for an opening; that's usually the last thing that happens before management and HR formally offer the role to someone else within the company or have someone lined up externally. It's too late by then.

Go to the people you want to work with, express an interest in exploring the possibility of working with them when an opportunity arises and keep in touch. Get ahead of the curve so that you are the first to be considered.

Choice #4: Reach out to new employers

Sometimes, the problems don't go away. They are complex, systemic and it's outside your ability to change things. This is the time to **switch** from *Problem Vale* to *New Town* in the right job. Switch to a mindset of full ownership. Take control of your thoughts, feelings and actions, and in doing so, you will take control of your career and life.

Decide on what matters to you, recognise what employers want, and define and pursue your ideal job. This is the job where you get the things that are most important to you. You are well rewarded, have the opportunity to succeed, are surrounded by a great team, the work is interesting and you could become an expert, which will give you a sense of purpose.

The four mistakes people make

Here are the four mistakes people make that prevent them from finding and getting the right job.

Mistake #1: Being too busy and lacking clarity

Most people tend to pack more into the day than it is possible for them to complete, and the weekends can be more of the same. And why not? We live full lives.

The problem is that when things change at work – and they will – **you need to change with those changes.** If there is new management or financial instability, you need to be prepared to adapt to these changes.

When I ask people, 'What are the top three things you want in your next job?' do you know what the answer often is? Most people respond with 'That's a good question' or 'I haven't thought about it'.

This is your job and career, and considering so much hangs on it, you must make the time to gain clarity.

It's worth noting that when people are actively looking to change jobs, they can find that new opportunities look more interesting than ever. If you aren't clear on what you want, you could easily pursue and accept a job without considering what the right job may be for you, or what else is out there that could be a better fit for you. It's essential to own, discover and define the right fit for you.

Mistake #2: A boring resume and uninspiring LinkedIn profile

At times I look at resumes and wonder, 'How did you get this far without learning how to write persuasively and communicate with impact?' This is an essential criterion for professionals and managers.

Most resumes talk about job responsibilities (yawn) rather than results and success metrics in the face of significant challenges. They read like a tour of an art gallery rather than a James Bond blockbuster. And most times, when the average resume and LinkedIn profile gets the seven-second browse or scroll, James Bond will get the attention even though the art gallery might offer far more substance.

A lot of people dust off their old resume, put a few lines about their latest role and send it off – big mistake. Just as you are dynamic, so your resume should be too. You are likely to have learned more, achieved more and become more during your latest period of employment, so why do the basic update? It's better to take stock of who you are today, what you want from your next role, and create your career-marketing materials to communicate your current value proposition.

Mistake #3: Being passively open to opportunities

The problem with only exploring the few opportunities that come your way, is that you can spend the limited time you do have on those that may not be exactly what you want. And if you haven't made the time to get clarity and focus on the type of role and companies that are a good fit for you, you risk taking the wrong role. More than ever before, hiring managers and recruiters are under pressure to fill roles, so they could potentially over-sell the role. Often, I get calls and messages from people saying that their new job isn't what they were promised.

I'd suggest focusing on targeted opportunities by title, industry and company. Rather than being passively open to anything remotely relevant, proactively focus on roles and companies you really want to join. In this way, you can invest the limited time and energy you have on pursuing the right job and put everything into it to win it.

Mistake #4: Not sharpening your sword

Often, people tell me about the golden opportunity they had to interview with a company they really wanted to work with, but they bombed at the interview. 'Should've, would've, could've' statements abound afterwards.

Some people can walk right into interviews with minimal preparation. Others feel awkward and self-conscious, which results in them forgetting essential information that would have differentiated them from the other candidates. Some speak at a high level when the interviewer is expecting specific information, resulting in a mismatch of communication styles. And then there are the people who make the mistake of getting down to business too quickly, skipping the all-essential rapport-building stage which ensures mutual connectivity, a sense of common ground and maximum cooperation.

Interviews can be unpredictable so it's best to sharpen your sword by brushing up on your interview skills and go in prepared to build rapport. Give and get information to establish a strong MVP.

The Switch Method solution

The Switch Method offers a four-step solution that helps people to avoid these four major mistakes and get the right job. If you follow it sequentially, this model will help you to find clarity about what's right for you, build a personal brand that's attractive, get in front of the right audience and become the preferred person for the job.

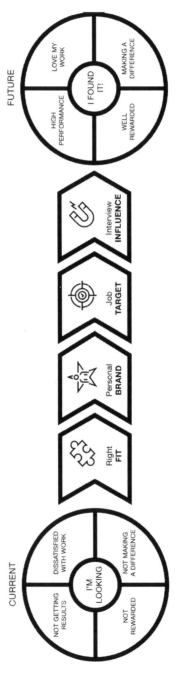

FUTURE

LOVE MY WORK

MAKING A DIFFERENCE

I FOUND IT!

HIGH PERFORMANCE

WELL REWARDED

Interview **INFLUENCE**

Job **TARGET**

Personal **BRAND**

Right **FIT**

CURRENT

DISSATISFIED WITH WORK

NOT MAKING A DIFFERENCE

I'M LOOKING

NOT GETTING RESULTS

NOT REWARDED

The Switch Method

Step 1: Decide on the right fit

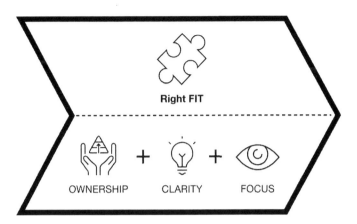

You know yourself best, so you must be clear about your right job fit. Where can you be successful, happy, rewarded and make a difference? To find the right fit, invest in these factors:

- Ownership: take control of the need to change and reach out for what you want

- Clarity: engage in a process of reflection, self-discovery and assessment to know and understand yourself

- Focus: get focused on the right fit, remove distractions and set goals about what you want from your next job in terms of role, culture, compensation and growth opportunity

The result at Step 1: you switch from confusion to clarity and focus on the right fit.

Step 2: Rev up your personal brand

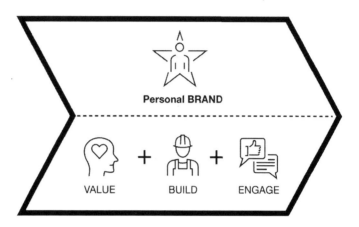

People who are visible in their organisation, industry and on social media tend to be more valued and compensated, and have more flexibility and opportunities for growth. To create a great personal brand, invest in these factors:

- Value: recognise the value you possess and be willing to promote yourself

- Build: create an impressive set of career-marketing materials

- Engage: grow and engage your network to maximise your influence

The result at Step 2: you switch from being ignored or forgotten to standing out and being socially promi-nent.

Step 3: Select the right employer and job target

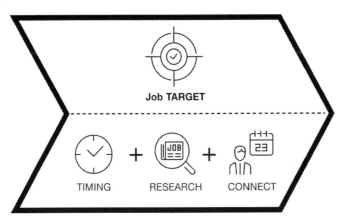

Often, people struggle to get interviews for the right role with the right companies at the right time. Similarly, companies struggle to find the right candidate when there is an opening. A targeted job search ensures you have the best chance of connecting with the right company for the right role. To succeed in this, invest in these factors:

- Timing: determine when it is time to start exploring new career opportunities

- Research: create a list of relevant companies and contacts to approach

- Connect: reach out to your target list, getting their attention and securing interviews

The result at Step 3: you switch from being one of many to being noticed and relevant.

Step 4: Interview to influence your way to success

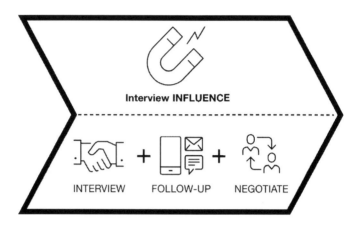

Interview INFLUENCE

INTERVIEW   FOLLOW-UP   NEGOTIATE

A well-suited candidate can miss out on a great role because they lack good interview and follow-up skills. Knowing how to interview well and follow up afterwards will maximise your chances. To succeed in this, invest in these factors:

- Interview: learn how to build rapport, discover client problems, challenges and desired results, and communicate how you can help the company achieve its goals

- Follow up: review the interview, assess the fit and decide whether or not to pursue and follow up the next steps to create momentum and maximise influence

- Negotiate: learn to align on outcomes and influence to reach agreement

The result at Step 4: you switch from being ineffective to being influential, preferred and offered the job.

Now that you know what The Switch Method is and the process involved, I recommend you assess what step you are at right now. We will cover the four steps of The Switch Method in the next four sections, starting with the first step: finding the right fit for you.

SECTION TWO
RIGHT FIT

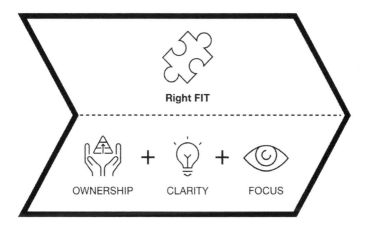

Right FIT

OWNERSHIP + CLARITY + FOCUS

THREE

The Mindset Of Ownership

PRINCIPLE

Switch from being a prisoner of others' choices to being the master of your destiny.

If you hate Mondays, *you are in the wrong job.* Some people hate Monday, celebrate hump day on Wednesday and have checked out by Friday. They have the Sunday night blues as they start thinking about work, reviewing their calendars and inboxes, and dreading the week ahead. And yet they go back to the same job, week in and week out.

A recent Gallup study of nearly 7,500 full-time employees found that 23% reported often or always feeling burned out at work, while an additional 44%

reported feeling burned out sometimes.[1] Another report found that 51% of people at work are not engaged and 16% are actively disengaged.[2]

People spend more time planning their holiday than their career. Some plan their holidays at work, but would never plan their career on holiday. They are stuck in the wrong job, unhappy, frustrated or burned out because they haven't challenged the status quo. They haven't asked themselves questions like 'Should I remain in this job?' or 'Is this role/manager/company the right fit for me?' And of course, they haven't acted on the obvious answer: **change something at work or change your work.**

Then there are those who make a different choice. They take ownership and make a conscious decision to look for jobs and build the career most people *WISH* for, where they are:

1. **Well** rewarded for their contribution

2. **Impacting** their colleagues, loved ones, community and the world

3. **Successful** in solving problems and achieving results

4. **Happy**, satisfied and have a sense of wellbeing

1   Wigert B and Agrawal S, 'Employee Burnout, Part 1: The 5 Main Causes', *Gallup, U.S.A.*, 12 July 2018, www.gallup.com/workplace/237059/employee-burnout-part-main-causes.aspx
2   Cobalt Community Research, 'Managing Community Engagement', not dated, www.cobaltcommunityresearch.org/managing-employee-engagement.html [accessed 16 January 2020]

SWITCH TIP

You will do your best work and live your best life by taking ownership of the choices and changes you are willing to make to get to your desired future.

Taking ownership

We are motivated to work to meet our deepest needs. When these needs aren't met, it leads to boredom at one end of the spectrum and burnout on the other, so it is essential we gain awareness of our needs and take an inventory of which ones are being met or not being met in our lives.

The Needs Pyramid

These needs can be grouped into five different levels. This may look familiar to you as it reflects ideas from Abraham Maslow's Hierarchy of Needs[3]; however these five levels in my model refer directly to employment needs.

Level 1: need to survive. This is the first and most basic need that gets people to work. We need an appropriate income to pay for food, housing, travel, education and clothing based on our life situation, phase, preferences and choices.

Level 2: need to thrive. This is the need for harmony and work-life balance. It requires a secure and stable environment for work and health, and flexibility in work and life. It also requires the ability to resolve problems at work, recover from setbacks, develop resilience and build strength. The need to thrive is the need to enjoy work, to find it interesting and engaging, and the availability of resources to perform a job well.

Level 3: need for tribe. This is the need for people with whom to collaborate to accomplish work. A single person does not build a skyscraper or a highway; we need a team. This team needs to be aligned with the goals, care, communication, support and respect of its team members. The tribe has its rituals and routines, and inspires loyalty, affinity, goodwill and a shared identity. It has a way of getting things done, and the team is better together.

---

3   Maslow, Abraham, 'A Theory of Human Motivation', Psychological Review, 50(4), 1943, pp370-96

Level 4: need for mastery. This is the need to be the best and achieve the most we are capable of. It is the purest expression of our abilities, matched with challenging opportunities, that produces results, and we need to have these results recognised and rewarded. We know we are at our best and have done our best at this level when we have opportunities for continuous development – to learn, act, fail, succeed and iterate. This offers us the chance to grow and develop our beliefs, thinking, ability and personality.

This level of need also offers us the chance to be the expert, trail blazer, innovator, authority, thought leader, evangelist – in other words, the most prominent voice among our peers and in our industry.

Level 5: need for purpose. This is the need for maximum fulfilment of self through our impact on the world – a need to meet others' needs, especially the people we care about, and make a significant contribution to society. This level offers us the ability to create a legacy and influence the generations to come, which fulfils the need to integrate the sum total of what we have accomplished through Levels 1–4 and make a positive difference in the lives of others. The need for purpose leverages all our resources and creates a better future for everyone we care about, helping them survive, thrive, find a tribe, achieve mastery and purpose.

> **SWITCH ACTION**
>
> Where are you now? Identify where you are on this stairway and what the next level looks like. As you consider new job opportunities, see if they offer you the chance to achieve every level on the stairway that matters to you.

The mindset of ownership means that you decide if your needs are or aren't being met. You are the one who is going to do what it takes to ensure that they *are met* within your current company or beyond. The benefits of taking ownership are:

1. You have clarity about what you are and aren't in control of, and are at peace with it

2. You aren't waiting for someone else to change things, which can be disempowering

3. You will do your best to make choices and change things you are in control of, which is empowering

The power equation: ownership > effect

When you are on the left side of this equation (ownership), you are in control of your thoughts, feelings and actions. You have the power to change your situation. When you are on the right side of the equation (effect), you are not in control and allow others to have an inappropriate influence over your thoughts, feelings, actions and quality of life.

Which side of the equation are you on? Who is driving the bus of your life?

Is it you or others? Are you owning your life, or are you living influenced by the effects of others' decisions? When people are influenced by the effect of other people's actions or forces outside their control, they make statements like:

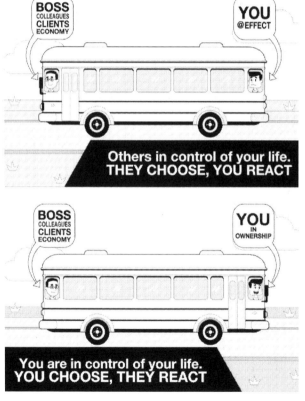

Who is driving the bus of your life?

- They promised me a raise a year ago, and I'm still waiting

- There's this person on my team who's constantly taking credit for my work

- The company is struggling financially, and I'm hoping someone is going to do something about it

- They make me work long hours, and nobody cares about the effect it has on me

- My work is boring and has no purpose, but there aren't any jobs out there, so I might as well just soldier on

When you are at the 'effect' of your manager and colleagues, it will result in a growing sense of anger, sadness, guilt, shame, helplessness, frustration and regret. If this is ongoing, it will impact every other area of your life. It's essential to move from the **effect** to the **ownership** side of the equation, and to do so, you need to start by becoming aware of your self-limiting beliefs and decisions.

The ownership checklist

Read each statement below and decide on the answer that describes what you believe. You can find the template for this checklist at www.switch.work/bonus

- I am in charge of my choices, my successes and failures. Yes/no

- I am clear about what I want in my job and my career. Yes/no

- I can choose the people I work with and how they impact the quality of my work. Yes/no

- I choose the manager I work with as much as they choose me. Yes/no

- I embrace failure as feedback and work on succeeding. Yes/no

- I initiate actions to change my circumstances if they don't meet my needs. Yes/no

- I can find the right job that meets my needs when I look for it. Yes/no

- I am the best version of myself at work. Yes/no

- I am creating my future with every decision I make and action I take. Yes/no

Each question that you answered yes to is a self-empowering belief. These *accelerate your progress* towards your goals.

Each question that you answered no to or were undecided on is a self-limiting belief. These *prevent you* from reaching your goals.

Self-awareness about empowering and limiting beliefs is powerful. Once you become aware of what is holding you back, you can take action to deal with this hand-brake and move forward without anything stopping you. You can **change your self-limiting beliefs**

to self-empowering ones; this can be difficult, but it is possible and you will enjoy the benefits for the rest of your life.

In the context of your work and career, empowering beliefs will help you stand out, be preferred and get the job that is right for you.

Self-limiting decisions and beliefs

Self-limiting decisions and beliefs are negative, oppositional to your abilities and prevent you from achieving your highest potential. They are ideas that you developed through a single major incident or a series of small events or words spoken to you about your abilities and potential. Often, they were installed during childhood, teen years or early adult life, but they will affect decisions you make for the rest of your life unless you consciously recall them, review them and change to positive, self-empowering beliefs.

In days gone by, circus staff would train baby elephants to stay in one place by chaining one of their legs to a tent pole. At first, the baby elephant would pull at the chain, but it couldn't walk away. It would try again and again, but as the weeks went on, it would stop trying. The elephant would decide it did not have the strength to break free. And as it grew up, it wouldn't try to break free from the chain and the pole because it believed that it couldn't.

Baby elephants weigh 200 kg (440 lb), but when they are fully grown, they can end up being ten to twenty-five times that weight – a staggering 2,000–5,000 kg (4,400–11,000 lb). At this weight, the elephant could easily break the chain or the pole. In fact, it could pull down the whole tent! Yet the grown elephant believes it can't.

The point of this story is simple. Over time and as a result of a series of consequences, the elephant had decided that the chain was too strong for it, which was accurate when it was a baby. But that decision became a *limiting belief*, preventing it from testing its strength as it grew older and breaking free, which it was fully capable of doing as an adult.

Essentially, a belief is an idea that we have accepted at a point in time through a series of repeated reinforcements. We likely all have moments in the past where we have compared ourselves with others and decided that we weren't good enough, smart enough or strong enough. These beliefs can remain with us for years or even a lifetime and prevent us from breaking free from limitations that have been imposed on us by ourselves or others.

Here are some of the limiting beliefs I hear from people around me every day:

- I can't speak confidently to a room full of people
- I'll never get that position

- She is the smart one in the family

- I can't ask for that promotion

- They will never give me a raise

- Why bother, I never get selected

- I'm just not ready

- I don't have the energy

- It's too hard to change

- I'll never have enough

- People won't like the real me

- There's no point in trying

- I can't stick to a plan

- There's nothing I can do about it

- It's too risky to change jobs

SWITCH ACTION

Consider the list above and make a note of any phrases that you have caught yourself saying or thinking.

The sad thing is that most of these beliefs are decisions we made about ourselves a long time ago. In most cases, they're not true any longer, but because we believe they are true, they affect our feelings, thoughts and choices on a daily basis, years later.

SWITCH TIP

You are stronger, wiser and more capable than you have ever been in the past. The information you have received, the skills you have developed and your experiences have changed you, whether you realise it or not.

Self-empowering decisions and beliefs

Empowering beliefs are positive, progressive and most importantly *possible*. They are ideas that will enable you to act on and reach any goal you set yourself. They will help you live each day and embrace challenges with confidence and positive expectation.

SWITCH TIP

It is critical to cultivate empowering beliefs like friends. They are friends to your future.

Here are some of the empowering beliefs I hear from people around me every day:

- I can learn any skill I want to

- I'm going to learn how to confidently speak to a room of people

- I've told my manager I'm interested in applying for the position

- I've asked for feedback so I can develop my skills to be a manager

- I've asked my manager to reassess my compensation, based on my results

- I'm going to keep trying until I have the opportunity to work on a project like that

- I'm ready and willing

- I will find the strength to get it done

- I can change

- I can earn to my full potential

- People will have to accept me for who I am

- I can do anything I choose

- I have all the resources I need

- There are plenty of opportunities out there

SWITCH ACTION

Reflect on the list above and make a note of any of the phrases that you have caught yourself saying or thinking.

You can change limiting beliefs into empowering beliefs. Beliefs are created at a moment in time when you decide that they are true, through your own judgement or someone else's. Either way, they can affect how you think, speak and behave for the rest of your life, so it's important to trace back a limiting decision in your memory to the moment it was formed. Assess whether it's still valid. If it's not, reject it and replace it with an empowering belief.

Reinforcing and building empowering beliefs will help you do your best work and live your best life.

SWITCH ACTION

Having completed this chapter, write down at least one thing you have learned and one action you need to take. You may like to use the Switch actions sheet at www.switch.work/bonus to record your learning points and action plan.

FOUR

Clarity About Your Sweet Spot

PRINCIPLE

Switch from confusion to a high-definition vision of your future.

> 'Pree, I've just left a company after a number of years and I'm looking for a new job. I could do a number of different roles, but I'm not sure what I should do. I've just not had the time to think about this.'

Most people say they have been too busy to figure out what they really want. They are unconsciously going through the motions without the self-awareness of what is and isn't important to them.

It's a bit like driving to a familiar place every day. You aren't necessarily thinking about the drive; more often than not, you are thinking about something else. How often do you notice the other cars on the road and the people around you? It works well when you are going to the same place every day, but if you need to drive someplace new, you will need to pay attention to the road in a highly conscious state.

It's the same when you want to change jobs. Become clear about where you want to go, and then actively figure out how to get there.

SWITCH TIP

Where attention goes, energy flows.

The importance of alone time

Since 2006, I have been writing in a journal and ensuring I get time alone early in the mornings before the kids wake up. To be honest, the regularity of this 'alone time' can vary from two to four days a week, and can fizzle out completely if we have been binge watching Netflix the night before, so there have been times when I've gone for a couple of weeks without my alone time.

For me, the tell-tale signs that I haven't been setting aside my reflection and journaling time include feeling overwhelmed, frustrated and occasional mild anxiety. When I get back into my routine, the result is like taking in 100% of my full lung capacity of fresh air. I can honestly say that this has become one of the most precious times in my day and has helped me to:

- Become more observant, conscious and intentional

- Understand people and problems a lot better

- Become aware of my strengths, weaknesses, preferences and dreams

- Have serendipitous moments and make startling discoveries

- Make great decisions at work and at home, and with my health and finances

- Live a life I am satisfied with and share it with the ones I care most about

- Achieve clarity about my life's purpose

We may not have the motivation of Steve Jobs, who trekked the Himalayan Ashrams in India for seven months, barefoot and dressed in a lungi (a traditional garment worn around the waist and extending to the ankles) for the purpose of solitude and enlightenment. But we all have the ability to create time to be alone and reflective each week.

Resist the common misconception that time to be alone and reflect is a 'guilty pleasure' – it is *especially* important if you have a busy home with kids and a demanding job.

This time helps you to be your best self to everyone else. Yes, it is one more thing on the list, but make it an intentional practice. The benefits will be enhanced self-awareness, problem solving, creativity, intuition and empathy. Most importantly, you will be on the road to greater clarity.

You can find thirty journaling prompts to achieve clarity and eight ways to be alone and reflective at www.switch.work/bonus.

The sweet spot of work (and life)

When I think of the thousands of interviews I have conducted, I find that successful people are clear about what matters to them and what doesn't. And they use this clarity as a guiding criterion early on in their job-search process. The most well rewarded, successful, happy and impactful people have answers to these four questions:

- **Clarity of expertise:** what am I good at?

- **Clarity of energy:** what do I love doing?

- **Clarity of reward:** what will the market pay me well to do?

- **Clarity of impact:** how can I make a difference with my loved ones, community and the world?

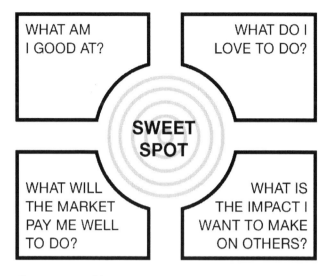

Sweet spot grid

SWITCH TIP

Clarity with action accelerates success and satisfaction.

Clarity of expertise

This is the first area of gaining clarity and should not be too difficult to define given that most of us work in jobs with clear metrics and feedback systems for success and failure. We tend to figure ourselves out through life's experiences, comments and feedback from people around us, as well as the results from our endeavours.

To gain clarity in terms of what we are good at and our area/s of expertise, we need to dig deeper and drill down to the core of what makes us uniquely who we are. Understanding our strengths and weaknesses, our knowledge, skillset and personality will bring clarity and definition.

To gain more clarity, here are a few questions to think about. I recommend you use your alone time to journal your responses:

- What are the most successful jobs you have had to date?

- Why did you succeed in them?

- What are you naturally good at, better than most around you?

- What topics do people ask you about for advice?

- What do people say about you – compliments, endorsements, referrals and job references?

Personality and behavioural preferences

Personality includes the notable characteristics of a person such as their mental, emotional, constitutional and social make up. These distinctive personality traits or characteristics will mean that some people are suited to certain tasks and jobs, while others are suited to different roles.

For example, highly patient people can be good at HR jobs or customer-service roles, but may struggle in the sales profession. On the other hand, those who have a bias for immediate action (and low patience) tend to struggle in accounting jobs, yet excel in trading and the stock markets. People who are curious and open to new opportunities are likely to enjoy success in exploratory and scientific fields, whereas those who like predictable and consistent work are great at quality assurance roles. People who are highly agreeable will tend to struggle making unpopular decisions as managers, whereas those who are comfortable with confrontation will excel in transformational roles.

Personality tests combine your responses and assess them in relation to choices made by millions of other people. These data sets analyse and bring to light trends in your behaviour and preferences that you may know to an extent, but are not fully aware of, especially if they are not what you consider desirable characteristics.

Of course, there are always benefits and drawbacks to any assessment tools. The disadvantage of personality tests is that they may ignore certain aspects, depending on the traits they're mapping and measuring. But the advantage of personality tests is that they help you to understand yourself better by providing insight into aspects of how you're wired. Understanding your specific personality traits, combined with insights about your key strengths and knowledge, is fascinating and powerful for gaining clarity of purpose.

Strengths and natural abilities

Your strengths are your natural abilities – those things in which you excel. They can loosely include your experience, values and skills, but for the sake of clarity here, let's go with strengths being your innate abilities.

Knowing your strengths and weaknesses can be immensely useful in a process of decision making about whether a role or career choice is right for you. This doesn't only apply when you're starting out in jobs and on the career path; it applies to every stage of this journey. In fact, it is more important as you navigate the upward trajectory from entry level management through mid-level to senior management.

The character strengths of perseverance and patience work extremely well in roles that are challenging, when your efforts may take months or sometimes years to yield fruit. On the other hand, a bias for action can be extremely useful in a role that requires decisiveness in ambiguous situations, building relationships with key clients and winning new customers.

Knowledge and experience

Knowledge incorporates skills, education and experience. This is the domain where qualities like insight, achieving specific results and problem solving can differentiate you significantly.

For example, growing a team or division that is successful in the face of obstacles makes you stand out. In the same way, if you have experience in leading a business unit through a financial crisis, that can be invaluable. And completion of an MBA program can also help you differentiate yourself in a competitive selection process for a sought-after leadership position.

It is critical to first recognise and then communicate what you are good at, to your future manager and those around you. This is what will encourage them to risk their reputation and make an investment in choosing you over the competition.

Clarity of energy

There's a saying I hear over and over again: 'All work and no play makes Jack a dull boy'. Unfortunately, this statement is often the reality for people who are overworked, time-poor and relationally bankrupt. They seldom renew and refresh to the extent that they need. Fun, enjoyment, down-time and flow-state are all luxuries relegated to weekends or the annual family holiday, and when these people come back to 'the grind', the down-time becomes but a distant memory.

I believe that we need to find the things and people that energise us at work itself. To gain more clarity, here are a few questions to think about and journal:

- What energises you at work?

- What have you loved about your last three jobs?

- What have you hated about your last three jobs?

- What do you look forward to at work?

- If you were not afraid to fail, what would you do for work?

SWITCH TIP

When you give priority to activities and people that you value, it will energise you.

The prevailing mindset I grew up with was that you choose a profession that is secure, pays well and has opportunities to step up the corporate ladder. There was certainly no place to seriously pursue any passions you might have like music or sport; you could always do those as a hobby, but they were not considered to be real jobs. This mindset meant that people were never encouraged to think about what they might love to do at work – work that would engage them, challenge them, make them lose track of time.

Fortunately, times have changed in terms of people pursuing their passions in a work setting. But for many of us, there is still the challenge of defining what it is we love and enjoy doing, what motivates and energises us, and pursuing it with clarity.

Whether we realise it or not, our passion, motivation, interests and goals are closely tied to our values. Values are attributes or qualities that we admire, prefer and desire for ourselves. They are powerful forces at work in our lives that can create happiness and success, as well as dissatisfaction and disengagement. Most people can tell me two or three things that they value in the context of work, but few people have a high degree of clarity and the certainty that comes from values that they have identified and validated.

SWITCH TIP

It is essential to become conscious of your values and use them as a guiding force in your life to explore new opportunities and identify what is right for you.

It's your responsibility to do the work of identifying your values, and once you have, to validate them with your spouse, partner, loved ones and friends. You then need to ensure you communicate them to your managers, peers, business partners, customers, recruiters, current colleagues, past colleagues and anyone else who may influence and have an impact on your career. This will reduce the 'values friction' that you can experience when working with people who have a different set of values from yours. It will also help reduce the likelihood of job dissatisfaction, failure and frequent searching for new opportunities.

It's about **making your priorities a priority.** A values-driven person will develop a career shaped by decisions that are guided by their values and determine whether their current or prospective employer and role are the **right fit** for them.

Clarity of reward

This is the third area of gaining clarity. Since money and financial reward are a means to other things – enabling a lifestyle, choices and freedom – the one caution I make is not to change jobs just to make more money. It's understandable at an early stage of your career, where a $10–$15,000 a year raise can be life changing, but at a mid to senior level, after taxes, you won't even notice the difference. You need to consider all the other clarity areas to ensure you have the ability to succeed, enjoy your work and make a difference in addition to the financial rewards.

To gain more clarity, here are a few questions to think about and journal:

- How satisfied are you with what you earn today?

- What are the things you would like to invest in, afford and experience that are not possible at your current level of income?

- What would you need to learn, improve or change to go to the next level of income?

- How much of an improvement would make a noticeable difference to your life?

- What are the other aspects of benefits and reward that are important to you?

SWITCH TIP

The real issue to be aware of when changing jobs is whether there's a mutual exchange of value between you and your employer.

What's your market value? Does your compensation make you feel like your contribution is valued? I recommend using money as a criterion for change when one or more of these circumstances arise:

- You aren't being recognised for delivering above and beyond results.

- You have raised the issue of money with your manager and employer, but it has not yielded the results you wanted.

- You have grown within the ranks and your salary has not been equivalent to your increase in responsibilities and title.

- You are certain and have validated that you are paid 20% less than the industry average for your position with other companies.

- There is a significant discrepancy between you and your peers because they negotiated better deals when they joined the company.

- You have explored the possibility of growing within the organisation to no avail. Growth and promotion are easier to achieve internally because you have proven yourself. They bring an increase in compensation, which should be market tested. Treat this the same as accepting a job externally.

- Managers have made and then broken promises in relation to compensation.

- The bonus and incentive structures are too complex and difficult to achieve.

What are your salary expectations? Here are some options to consider:

1. Growth

This is the first and most popular option. The cost of living continues to rise. People's needs continue to grow, and since income is a measure of reward and value, most people want an improvement in their compensation package. At a minimum, you would expect a 15%–20% increase to keep up with the cost of living three years from now, especially if you intend to take on new expenses like buying a house or an investment property, putting your children through university or maximising your financial position at retirement.

Assess what you would be getting paid for a similar position elsewhere within your industry, and for a level up if you are ready for and seeking a promotion. It is essential to keep in mind that an improved salary could come with a higher level of responsibility and stress, additional work hours and a new company culture. Ensure that the increase is worth the change. Be clear about what would make it worth it and boldly ask for this.

2. Match

The second option is matching your current compensation. A number of people feel like their need for compensation is met, but other important areas, like being good at their work, finding the work and culture enjoyable and making an impact beyond themselves, are severely lacking. This is a good reason to consider upgrading to jobs where you will succeed, find the work engaging and the culture suitable, and meaningfully impact on the world. Before making the choice to move laterally for money, carefully measure the difference in the other areas and validate it with other people.

3. Reduce

The third option is to take a step back in compensation. This is the least favoured option, but people do choose it when their gain in other areas, such as being good at their job, loving their work and making an impact in the world, is overwhelmingly appealing.

Clarity of impact

This is the fourth and final area of clarity. Companies are becoming increasingly aware of the fact that many employees want to support a variety of initiatives, so that they see their work and workplace as having an impact and meeting the needs of the world around them.

To gain more clarity, here are a few questions to think about and journal:

- What causes move you the most?

- Why do they matter to you?

- How would you like to be able to make a difference through your life and work?

- If you didn't need to work, how would you spend your time helping others?

- When all is said and done, what would you want people to say about you?

Impactful initiatives can include sponsorship, fund-raising, workplace giving, volunteering and donation of expertise and goods. Increasingly there are people who are successful, happy and well rewarded complaining that something is missing in their lives – this is the ability to have an impact in the lives of others and is a welcome change from self-centred living to others-centred living. People want to make a difference and live beyond themselves, particularly in these spheres of influence: loved ones, the community and the world.

Loved ones include our families, friends and the people we care deeply about. From extended paternity and maternity leave through to colleagues rallying around a co-worker who has a child with a terminal illness or who has experienced sudden tragedy, the teams with the best cultures rise to the occasion when those around them are hurting.

The community includes local and professional groups that we participate in. Today, thanks to social groups online, this extends across continents where people are connected via technology and ideas that unite them. People who are engaged in their tribe or community and serve within them report a greater sense of wellbeing.

The world includes global-level causes focused on environmental, political and social issues, and their impact on the future. We can all be a voice for and an active supporter of some of the world's greatest issues, as well as helping to raise awareness within our communities and among our loved ones. There is so much need out there.

In September 2015, the UN's General Assembly adopted the '2030 Agenda for Sustainable Development' which includes seventeen sustainable development goals, from quality education to climate action.[1] Why not have a look and see which ones align with your values?

---

1   United Nations, 'Sustainable Development Goals', not dated, www.un.org/sustainabledevelopment/sustainable-development-goals [accessed 16 January 2020]

SWITCH TIP

We all care about something. We may not be able to change everything ourselves, but we can change some things and make a difference.

CATHERINE'S STORY: CAREERS AND BUSINESS AS A FORCE FOR GOOD

Catherine was a victim of the war atrocities committed by the Lord's Resistance Army (LRA), led by Joseph Kony, that ravaged Uganda. She, like many, had seen her parents killed in front of her eyes. She had been captured, enslaved and forced to commit inhumane and unspeakable acts of violence against other children. Many in these camps tried to escape, running for freedom – for every hundred that fled, fewer than five made it to safety. Most of the others were gunned down or recaptured and killed to set an example to the others in the camp.

Catherine found refuge in the Watoto villages of Northern Uganda which exist to rescue, raise and rebuild the lives of children like her. Founded by Gary and Marilyn Skinner, these villages consist of homes that house up to eight children with a mother who has been dislocated from her home and family. The mothers provide a loving environment where the process of healing and integration into a normal life can begin. The villages provide physical care, medical intervention, formal and vocational education, as well as moral and spiritual training, raising the children to become leaders who can bring sustainable change to their world.

After ten years of sponsorship, Catherine graduated with a Certificate in Polytechnic Studies and has transitioned into her adult life, self-sustained and pursuing her dreams.

Since 2006, my wife and I have sponsored Catherine, who is an adult now, and twenty-one others like her, some of whom are teenagers and one woman with HIV. About ten of them are at Watoto and the rest are spread across the continents of South America, Africa and Asia. We must meet others' needs, because we can.

I believe that our careers and businesses can become a force for good. There are so many needs right on our doorstep in our families, in our communities and in the world beyond. We can't solve every problem, but when we play a part in helping someone else achieve a better life and realise their dreams and hopes, we become a force for good.

Focus on the sweet spot of work

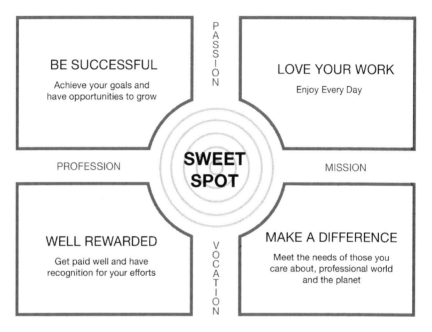

BE SUCCESSFUL

Achieve your goals and
have opportunities to grow

P
A
S
S
I
O
N

LOVE YOUR WORK

Enjoy Every Day

PROFESSION

**SWEET
SPOT**

MISSION

WELL REWARDED

Get paid well and have
recognition for your efforts

V
O
C
A
T
I
O
N

MAKE A DIFFERENCE

Meet the needs of those you
care about, professional world
and the planet

Focus on finding the sweet spot

As you become clear about what you are good at, love to do, get rewarded for and make a difference doing, you can focus your efforts towards the activities and jobs which align best with these areas. As you get closer to this, you will find the sweet spot of work and enjoy success and satisfaction in your passion, mission, vocation and profession.

- **Passion**: when you find what you are good at and love to do, you have discovered your passion

- **Mission**: when you find what you love that makes an impact on others, you have discovered your mission

- **Vocation:** when you find what makes a difference in the world and you can get paid for it, you have discovered your vocation

- **Profession**: when you find what you are good at that makes you money, you have discovered your profession

You may not find all four areas in one job, but it's important to take stock of what you have right now, and then seek to find that which is missing in your work. Assess each job opportunity you have before making a decision.

When you have work you are good at, love to do and can make money from, you will experience high levels of satisfaction. But if you're not having an impact on others, you can end up feeling like your life is not making a difference in the world, unless you find ways to have an impact outside of work.

When you have work you are good at, love to do and you're having an impact, you can experience fulfilment and job satisfaction. But if you don't make enough money to support the lifestyle you desire, it won't be sustainable in the long term, unless you find ways to supplement your income outside of work.

When you have work you love to do, you're making an impact and getting paid well, you can experience excitement and fulfilment. But if you aren't good at it, you will have a sense of uncertainty and lack confidence, unless you find ways to get good at it in an acceptable time frame.

When you have work you are good at, you're making an impact and getting paid well, you can experience a high degree of success and comfort. But if you aren't loving it and happy with it, you'll lack the energy to keep going and burn out, unless you find ways to discover something you do love about it.

Finding the **right fit** is possible when you take ownership of what you need to move towards it, achieve clarity and focus on alignment at work and, if needed, supplement what is missing in your activities outside of work.

SWITCH ACTION

Now you've completed this chapter, write down at least one thing you have learned and one action you need to take. You may like to use the Switch actions sheet at **www.switch.work/bonus** to record your learning points and action plan.

FIVE

Focus On Finding
The Right Fit

PRINCIPLE

Switch from misfit to the right fit.

It is essential to find the right fit between your true, authentic self and the work environment in which you can express it, and indeed excel in it. Authenticity is the extent to which you feel comfortable to be yourself in any setting, be it at home or work, with family, friends, work colleagues, clients etc. This is a critical factor for longevity, job satisfaction and most importantly your wellbeing. People who aren't comfortable with who they are, or feel that they have to be someone else, become disengaged and disconnected after a while, or can experience stress and burnout trying to be someone they are not in roles and work environments in which they don't fit.

We have our **adaptive self** and our **authentic self.** The adaptive self helps us to navigate challenging, difficult and unfamiliar situations. Its highest purpose is self-preservation and it protects us from getting hurt based on past experiences. If you don't like how you act in certain situations, it's worth exploring why you behave this way and whether your adaptive self is in operation.

The authentic self helps you to express yourself to be comfortable, whole and self-confident in who you are. I recommend seeking out people and environments where you can be your authentic self, and let your adaptive self navigate uncertain territory only when it is required, rather than full time.

SWITCH TIP

Congruence is the degree to which there is alignment between how you think and feel (on the inside), and how you talk and behave with others in public.

Part of being true to your authentic self is finding congruence in all settings. When the work you do aligns with your personal values and beliefs, and you can be your true self, you are more likely to remain in harmony for the best part of your day. Going a step further, you are more likely to set the right expectations with your reports, peers and managers because of this alignment.

Being congruent is not about walking around without a filter and telling everyone exactly how you feel about them (unless that's how you want to live and work). What I am saying is that how you behave should be in harmony with your thoughts and feelings. For example, if you don't like or get along with a peer, spend only as much time with them as is absolutely necessary to get the job done. If a manager in your organisation is making personal remarks or behaving in a manner that makes you feel uncomfortable, have the courage to tell this person and stand up for yourself.

In some cases, the manager you are working for may be blunt or direct by nature, not personally attacking you. It may be a case of learning to work with their type of personality, and that in itself can be personal growth. If, however, inappropriate behaviour continues and is not being adequately addressed by senior management, then seek opportunities to work elsewhere, either within or outside the organisation. But seek advice first from those who have your best interests in mind so that you make a fully informed decision.

SWITCH TIP

If you are exploring new job opportunities show up as your true self. That way you can never go wrong.

It's easy to figure out whether or not something is the right fit for you when you are being authentically you. If the conversation with a potential employer flows and you feel comfortable, even energised by the person or people you are talking to, it's likely to be heading in the right direction. Even in the face of potential challenges and obstacles, you are more likely to come out on the other side stronger if you have alignment with the team around you and a connection to the part you play in it.

On the other hand, if the person or people you are meeting with and talking to are too stiff or uninspiring, then you know you are probably not going to enjoy working with them. It's a simple hack, but it could have saved many from taking on jobs that were just not the right fit.

You + employer = fit

The most important equation in terms of exploring new opportunities is whether you and the employer are matched. I'm not talking about a 100% fit – this is too good to be true and may not even exist. I'm talking about a strong relevant potential to successfully work together due to a majority of factors that align.

Let's expand the concept of fit in relation to a potential role, manager, team and organisation. There are four areas that must have a strong fit for longevity and success:

- **Role fit**: this is where you have a set of skills and strengths that help you to excel in your role

- **Manager fit**: this is where you share a strong values alignment with your manager

- **Culture fit**: this is where you share a strong values alignment with your team and the overall organisation

- **Financial fit**: this is where the position offers compensation and reward that meet or exceed your needs

SWITCH TIP

The effect of finding the right fit between you and an employer will result in high levels of engagement, satisfaction and performance. This sets up a virtuous cycle of career success and growth.

Focus on setting and getting goals

I'm sure you have come across the SMART acronym for setting goals. They should be:

- Specific

- Measurable

- Actionable

- Realistic

- Timely

For the purpose of this chapter, SMART is a useful tool for focusing on finding the right fit for you in your work. But have you ever wondered *why* you should do it this way? Let's look first at the conscious and unconscious aspects of your mind to understand the why and what is going on.

You have a conscious and unconscious part of your mind, and each one plays a vital role in your day-to-day living. Your conscious mind is the part that observes, analyses and makes decisions. Your unconscious mind is the part that stores memories, runs your body, maintains habits and responds instinctively. It is the domain of your emotions and plays an important role, but most of the time you will be unaware of its influence on your body and its responses.

Have you ever had moments when you've realised you can't remember much, if anything, about a routine activity such as travelling a familiar route? You were probably preoccupied with other thoughts, so how did you know when to start, turn, stop and stay on route? When your attention is on other things, your conscious mind is preoccupied, but your unconscious mind is keeping you on course.

The moment you pay attention to or focus on something, you switch from operating out of your unconscious mind to your conscious mind. The conscious mind is what I call the **goal setter** and the unconscious mind is the **goal getter,** and together, I refer to these as the **power couple.**

SWITCH TIP

When your conscious mind and unconscious mind work together, you will achieve peak performance, the best results and the best life. Together they become your ultimate power couple.

Change and new behaviours start out as conscious processes, then become habits after repetition. They move from the realm of conscious choice (goal setter) to automatic unconscious behaviour (goal getter). Note that the decision to change is a conscious decision to set goals, which you need to do to ensure success.

If you think back to the time you first learned how to drive, you started with the **decision** and a sustained **desire**. The decision (goal setting) was made by your conscious mind and the desire (goal getting) was sustained by your unconscious mind. Do you remember how you learned to drive and the resources you required (eg car, instructor, time etc)? Gaining the skill was a combination of conscious and unconscious behaviour – decision and desire working together; goal setting and goal getting behaviour. You were conscious of the steering wheel, the gears, the speed, the instructions you were getting, and at first, you may have felt like you were speeding even though you weren't. But as time went by, you stopped noticing as much, and then you didn't have to think how to do it at all. The new behaviour became a habit. This learning was preserved by your unconscious mind, and then you knew how to drive.

Achieving goals using your conscious and unconscious mind

In the Ownership chapter of this section, I introduced you to the *Needs Pyramid* and the five different levels of needs you are motivated to fulfil – the need to survive, thrive, find a tribe, achieve mastery and purpose. If you are like four out of five people, your needs are not being met at work – you are dissatisfied or unhappy about something, but 'can't quite put a finger on it'. Something is 'just not right'. You might have negative emotions associated with your workplace which can cause anger, fear, sadness, regret and guilt to surface.

We all experience unresolved emotions stored in our unconscious mind. These are powerful forces and should be resolved without delay, otherwise they will continue to have a negative impact on us. It is essential to make a conscious choice about what you want to resolve, the change you desire and the goal you want to achieve. This is a combined use of your conscious and unconscious mind where you use the **power couple** to **set** and **get goals.**

Setting Goals SMARTly

Now you know the why behind goal setting and goal getting, I'll show you how I use the SMART framework for setting goals.

- **S** – **specific**: it must be something you want

- **M** – **measurable**: you must have evidence to show when you have it

- **A** – **actionable**: you must desire it and be in control of maintaining/achieving it

- **R** – **realistic**: it must be something that is achievable for you

- **T** – **timely**: it must be time specific

SWITCH ACTION

Referring to the table below, decide on your goal and, using the SMART framework, consider and record your responses to each of the questions. You may download a version of this SMART goals table from www.switch. work/bonus.

Smart Goals Table

Goal	What is my goal? Why do I want to achieve this?	
Specific	Who is involved? What resources do I need? Where will I do this?	
Measurable	What is my indicator or measure that I have achieved my goal?	
Actionable	What am I going to do to initiate, maintain and achieve my goal?	
Realistic	How realistic is it given my circumstances? Who else has achieved this?	
Timely	When will I get started? (Now?) By when will I complete this (eg within ninety days)?	

SWITCH ACTION

Once you have written down your SMART goal from Switch action 1, look at these examples of action you can take to fuel your desire so that your unconscious mind (goal getter) stays on track to achieve it:

- Find a few people who are trying to achieve the same or similar goal(s) and be accountable to each other (in person or online)

- Journal about your journey towards your goal

- Set up visual reminders in places you frequent about the desired outcome

- Do something every day towards achieving this goal

- Give yourself a negative consequence for not actioning your plans – deny yourself something you enjoy (eg coffee, chocolate, Netflix etc)

- Give yourself a positive consequence for actioning your plans

- Pick yourself up if you fall by the wayside and start over again

DANIEL'S STORY: FOCUSING ON THE RIGHT FIT

Daniel was a successful senior sales professional in a global technology company. He had developed a reputation for being highly dependable when it came to achieving his annual sales targets. In fact, for four years in a row, he'd exceeded his multimillion-dollar targets and earned well. In addition to a base salary of $150,000, he was earning $300–400,000 each year with commissions and benefits.

Being a top sales performer, he was asked regularly to help on-board and coach new sales people. This was positioned as an opportunity for him to move into management. He accepted the responsibility and completed an internal leadership training course he was recommended to attend.

In his fourth year of employment, he was made sales director – this was a big break for Daniel as he had focused on getting this role for a number of years. And now it was his.

At first, he enjoyed the opportunity to build a brand-new team. There were a lot of interviews, hiring new team members and accompanying them on sales visits. But as time went on, he noticed that not all of his sales people were equally motivated or talented. He invested more time into coaching and developing them, but he found that there was a predictable 'bell curve' pattern where 70% of his team achieved target, but 30% of the team did not. As a consequence, his team's results came in at 70%–80% of his previous targets.

Despite an increase in his base salary from $150,000 to $180,000 as a result of being promoted into management, Daniel ended up with a significant drop in total earnings. Around this time, his kids were about to finish school and there was the prospect of university fees ahead, so the decreased income was quite concerning. In addition, he was working much longer hours and managing many people.

He continued in the sales director's role for eighteen months, until one day it hit him – he wanted his work to enable him to make a difference in his kids' lives by being able to send them to university and spend more time with them before they became adults. But right now, what he was doing was just not working, so he made the decision to leave.

Daniel came to me and stated, 'My biggest problem is that I don't know what the right job is for me.' I asked him to spend some time by himself *and focus on finding the right fit.* Two weeks later, he called me and said he'd had an epiphany. He'd realised that he had been happiest being an experienced sales professional, working with a mid-sized company in an individual capacity. He didn't want the long hours, the stress of a needy team and, most importantly, missing out on maximising his earnings in his late forties. He decided there would be time later on if he wanted to return to a management career.

Daniel quit his job and went looking for what brought him satisfaction and happiness. He found the role he wanted. It took a while, but he has achieved his sales targets and the desired income. He has saved more for his kids' university education and has had more time to be around them – all because he acted and focused on the right fit for him.

SWITCH ACTION

Now you've completed this chapter, write down at least one thing you have learned and one action you need to take. You may like to use the Switch actions sheet at www.switch.work/bonus to record your learning points and action plan.

SECTION THREE
PERSONAL BRAND

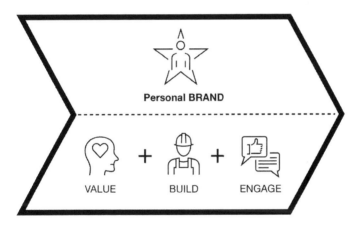

Personal BRAND

VALUE + BUILD + ENGAGE

SIX

Your Self-value Drives Market Value

PRINCIPLE

Switch from self-doubt to self-confidence.

Value yourself

In the previous section on **the right fit,** we focused on taking ownership to meet your needs, gaining clarity about what you're good at, love doing, get paid for and can do while making an impact on the world. This is essential to know, but moving forward, it's also important to recognise that employers have a lot of choice of available candidates, so mid to senior professional and management roles are highly competitive. You are competing with people in three categories: those seeking to **step up** into the level you desire from their current roles; those who wish to **side step** from the same level of role and responsibility in another company; and those who want to **step back** for a number of different reasons. You need to prepare to **stand out in a competitive job market.**

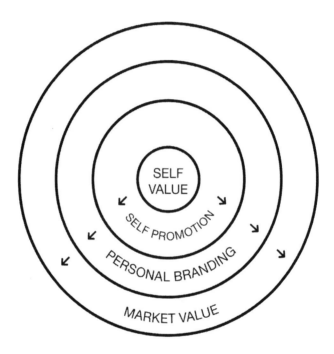

Self-value, market value

The benefit of standing out from the competition is that you become preferred and pursued. That increases your market value, ie what employers will offer you to come and work for them at your highest potential to solve their biggest problems.

To increase your market value, you need to be willing to build a high-profile socially visible personal brand. To build your brand, you need to confront and overcome any self-doubt and limiting beliefs about promoting yourself. If you aren't willing to promote yourself, you need to go to your core and recognise the value your possess. Your personal brand has to start with self-value.

A lack of self-value is a major problem that prevents you from going to the next level. It will slow down your progress and limit your career growth. This lack shows up in the workplace in the form of avoiding the spotlight, not attempting something for fear of failure and low confidence in your own abilities. It prevents you from stepping outside your comfort zone, which has a long-term ripple effect and results in missed opportunities, regret and frustration.

SWITCH TIP

You have a unique set of values, beliefs, skills, experiences and personality. This potent combination presents a distinct, remarkable person in the workplace.

As you go along in your career, you meet needs, solve problems, achieve goals and deliver results, which further shapes who you are. You learn from your mistakes, take failure as feedback and keep moving forward. Your future manager and employer needs someone like you – someone who has learned lessons – to solve their problems, achieve their goals and deliver results they care about. This is the *MVP* between you and your employer. For them to see the value you bring, you have to show it, and to show it, you have to be willing to promote yourself.

Fear of self-promotion will limit your career

For many people, self-promotion is a bad thing. They have seen the stereotypical narcissistic self-promoter who will stop at nothing to serve his or her own purposes and trample over everyone else to get to the top.

Having worked for two Fortune 500 companies for ten years, and then consulted to over 100 global companies, I have seen both extremes in self-promotion. Some people try too hard and go too far to promote themselves, which is undesirable at any time. This includes behaviours like bragging about themselves, putting other people down, hogging the limelight and taking every opportunity to push themselves forward.

You don't need to be that person.

At the other end of the spectrum, there are people who avoid the limelight and shrink back. They lack the courage and confidence to speak up when the situation requires it and there is a need for their voice.

The danger is that we can take extreme examples and, disliking certain traits in people, we may end up developing a **limiting belief** about self-promotion. We have developed the majority of our beliefs from our culture and upbringing. These are invaluable as long as they are **empowering beliefs.** If we see self-promotion as a bad thing, that kind of belief will prevent us from stepping up and standing out, both of which are absolutely essential in a career where the higher we go, the fewer the jobs and the greater the competition from others.

Self-promotion is the accelerator for your career success

Think of it this way: if the company you work for didn't promote itself, it wouldn't have customers and revenue and would close down. The best known brands in the world – Apple, Nike, McDonalds, Microsoft, Toyota and Disney, for example – have all made their way to the top by combining great value with self-promotion. Customers need to become aware of the value that these brands offer so that the brands can solve their problems and meet their needs.

You could also look at it like this: what if you decided to start a business or contract/consult on a daily rate to companies? How would you get clients to keep you in business? Self-promotion, of course.

You need to self-promote to achieve your highest potential with your career. Employers and industry executives need to become aware of the value you offer so that they can prefer and pursue you to solve their problems and achieve their goals.

SWITCH TIP

Self-promotion is not actually about you alone. It's about making others who have problems that you can solve aware of this.

The modern workplace is busier than ever with every possible digital tool connecting us (and disconnecting us). Hot desks, travel for work and flexible work-from-home options have changed how people connect with and recognise their immediate and extended peers and colleagues. It's easy to get lost in the crowd, and **your contribution will go unnoticed unless you bring it to people's attention.** It's not that people don't care; it's that they too are consumed with things that demand their attention. If you want to be recognised for your efforts, abilities and insight, you must be seen.

You can do this by sharing your opinions, expertise, accomplishments and results with others with **the purpose of helping them achieve the same as you, now or in the future.** It enables, encourages and inspires others when they see your success, and they can also learn from your mistakes. In addition, you can focus on the accomplishments and learnings that your team or department has achieved and become the chief advocate for them to recognise their efforts. This will foster better team work, build visibility for others and get the attention of your peers and management.

Your intention to promote others must be genuine, otherwise you will be found out sooner or later, but it is possible to promote others and yourself and build good public relations (PR). You could become the person who embraces the new direction the company is taking, putting your hand up for hot projects. Senior managers are always looking for people who are innovative, progressive and willing to champion a new project or direction.

Valuing yourself is the first step to being willing to share your personal brand with others. You have immense value to offer your peers, future managers, the industry and the world at large, and it is your responsibility to make this known. This builds your social capital, which in turns builds your personal brand. A strong personal brand will open opportunities you may not even have imagined before, and you can then choose to do work you love and are good at that pays well and meets the needs of the world.

SWITCH TIP

Without self-promotion, you will survive, but with self-promotion, you will thrive.

Value your social capital

At work, building great work relationships with colleagues, clients, partners and other influential people, is essential for career progression – it creates social capital. In person, you need to be seen and heard within the company as well as at industry events. Digitally, this means using tools such as LinkedIn to post articles, announcements and status updates, and connect with your current and past colleagues who remain within the industry ecosystem via social-media platforms.

Your visibility on LinkedIn, for example, will keep you top of mind, and as opportunities come up at your former colleagues' new workplaces, they will be encouraged and incentivised to refer you to hiring managers and recruiters. This creates an opening for these recruiters to approach you with career opportunities, preferring and pursuing you over others who don't have the same social capital.

SWITCH TIP

Social capital is essential for career progression.

The job market is more fluid than ever before with people being social, digital, mobile and willing to seize opportunities at a moment's notice. With terminations and redundancies so common in large corporations, loyalty is becoming less important as employees wake up to the fact that the **employer-employee relationship must be mutually valuable.** When it's not, one of the two parties will exit the relationship.

It is critical for you to build your social capital across the company with clients, partners, associates and industry recruiters as it's invaluable when you're looking at changing jobs, but this is often ignored in business schools and corporate training in general. Embracing your social capital and personal brand building will benefit you, your family and the world around you. Rejecting this could see you missing out on great jobs, getting increasingly frustrated and stuck in between jobs for a long time. I see it all the time. The hard truth is that most unsung heroes remain unsung. And the squeaky wheel does get oiled!

Value your personal brand

What do Elon Musk, Richard Branson, Arianna Huffington and Sheryl Sandberg all have in common? They are highly successful business leaders and they are known around the world. They could easily have been lost behind their well-known corporate brands, as many others have been. But these people are household names and often better known than Hollywood stars – because they have powerful *personal branding*. They are not only known by name, but people speak of them as if they know them personally – their personality, their failings, what they stand for etc.

These people are prolific on social and traditional media, and this helps them get noticed. It attracts opportunity and puts them top of mind for the fields they represent – Richard Branson for the Virgin Group of companies, Arianna Huffington for Thrive Global, Sheryl Sandberg for Facebook and Elon Musk for Tesla, SpaceX and SolarCity. They have chosen to cultivate and communicate with the world about their values, beliefs, vision, opinions and endeavours, and this has helped them build a personal brand and reputation in their field by which they have become memorable and mentionable. They have become distinct from their companies, too, so if they were to leave those companies, they would still be recognised, preferred and pursued.

These highly successful people all have a personal brand. I urge you to have one too.

SWITCH TIP

Personal branding is the key to influence.

I have sat in countless boardroom meetings when clients have been briefing me about recruiting a vice president, sales director, marketing director etc. Invariably, the names of people are mentioned – 'We want people like...' – and these generally fall into two categories. Firstly, they are people the executives have worked with, or someone in their team has worked with, who possess social capital. Secondly, they are people the executives see regularly on LinkedIn, posting articles, commenting on key issues and sharing photos of themselves and others at major industry events – ie the ones who are visible and have a **strong personal brand.**

This applies to people at every level of the organisation when it comes to career progression opportunities in an industry's ecosystem. Just because someone is a CEO, founder or business leader doesn't mean they automatically have strong personal branding – there are so many global companies whose leaders nobody knows.

SWITCH TIP

People work with people they know, like and trust. Personal branding helps you become known, liked and trusted. In essence, it helps you become the go-to person within your industry.

The ten benefits of building a personal brand

When you develop, define and build a compelling personal brand that employers notice, prefer, pursue and highly value, this happens:

1. You become known and distinct in people's minds for what you do

2. You get to showcase your strengths and passions

3. You get to choose who you want to work with and have greater influence in your workplace

4. Your satisfaction at work grows and you can enjoy your job

5. Your name is referred on to others as the person who is the best fit for a particular job/project/ team etc

6. You get approached for new opportunities that progress your career

7. You have the power to negotiate your ideal compensation and your income grows to meet your needs and desires, giving you more options and freedom

8. You are pursued, preferred, valued and appreciated

9. You become influential, and that influence benefits you and those you care about in countless ways for the rest of your life

10. Your career becomes a force for good

SWITCH TIP

A strong personal brand will make you preferred over your competition.

Your personal value proposition (PVP)

Developing and defining your PVP helps you build a compelling personal brand that employers notice, prefer, pursue and highly value. Your PVP is a promise to your future employer about the benefits they can expect to receive when they hire you – this is a current and future-facing promise. It is your sixty-second elevator pitch, and when you do it well, it can help you step up and stand out from the crowd.

You need to craft a compelling PVP to succeed. Here are the essential components:

- Who do you help? This is your target audience.

- What do you do? These are your strengths, skills and accomplishments.

- What benefit will the employer receive? This is the promise they get when employing you.

Your PVP should be scalable and consistent. It needs to suit the medium of communication and the attention span of the audience. This could look like:

- LinkedIn or resume headline in five to seven words

- An elevator pitch in twenty-five to fifty words

- A LinkedIn or resume summary in seventy to one hundred words.

- A direct approach message to a target employer in two hundred to two hundred and fifty words

You can find a PVP builder template and example at www.switch.work/bonus

The employer value proposition (EVP)

The EVP is the comprehensive value that the company offers you, comprising of (but not limited to):

- **Culture**: the people, values, work practices, social vibe, belonging, flexibility, diversity and inclusion

- **Leadership**: purpose, strategy, vision, mission, management style, challenges and social responsibility

- **Recognition**: compensation, incentives, benefits and awards

- **Growth**: training, development, opportunity, scalability and mobility

The EVP is what makes people want to stay with a company, and the lack of it makes people want to leave. The companies with a strong EVP tend to have happier employees who build great things, delivering high value to customers, which in turn leads to satisfied and loyal customers. This creates a virtuous cycle.

Once you have established that there is a need for your skills and experience through the formal process of a job application or the informal process of a referral, introduction or direct approach, you will meet with a variety of stakeholders through the interview the process. The key focus of your engagement is to help them understand your PVP and for you to understand their EVP.

The mutual value proposition (MVP)

The greater the affinity between the value you offer and the value the employer offers, the stronger the mutual value proposition (MVP). The MVP is the sweet spot where the PVP and the EVP are complementary – there is plenty of common ground and each party values what the other has. In sport, the analogies abound – it's where the star player finds a great team and an amazing coach, and the rest, as they say, is history.

The MVP is the partnership X-factor and ultimate objective of seeking a change in career jobs. Where there is a strong MVP and mutual appreciation between employer and employees, there is high performance, enjoyment of work, rewards and impact.

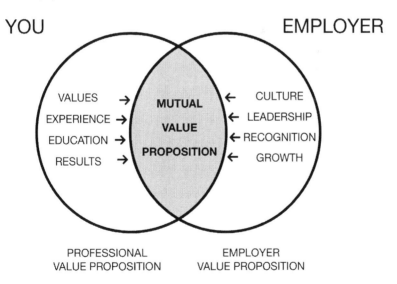

The mutual value proposition

Finding the MVP in your quest is not easy, but it is essential. That's why I believe you must take complete ownership of your career and reach out to connect and influence people across a number of potential opportunities. You will find the quality MVP role you are looking for if you are exploring a good quantity of roles at the beginning of your search. This reduces the fear of missing out on a particular role and allows you to be yourself and decide which roles to pursue to the next logical step.

It is your responsibility to recognise the MVP. When this is established, it helps you to work collaboratively with potential employers towards the highest common purpose and enable each other to achieve goals. When you find the MVP, it will allow you to thrive and become a force for good. This is essential to allow you to work with the right job and right team at the right time, and make great things happen.

SWITCH TIP

The best careers are built in the overlap of giving and getting what is important to each person.

In summary, when you value yourself and are willing to responsibly promote yourself to the target audience that needs what you do, you create your personal brand. This personal branding enables employers to notice, prefer, pursue and value you. The resulting MVP is the partnership X-factor where people are good at what they do, love their jobs, get well paid and make a difference in the world.

SWITCH ACTION

Having completed this chapter, write down at least one thing you learned and one action you need to take. You may like to use the Switch actions sheet at www.switch.work/bonus to record your learning points and action plan.

SEVEN

Build Your Personal Brand To Accelerate Your Career

PRINCIPLE

Switch from being lost in the crowd to standing out.

The Switch personal branding toolkit

Personal branding will light up your career. If you don't have a strong personal brand as you progress up the organisational pyramid, the chances are that when the senior jobs become fewer and more competitive, you will struggle to land your next job. Without a personal brand, you will be viewed as much like everyone else and risk getting passed over in the selection process.

To stand out, you must invest in building the career-marketing materials that help you to be seen and known in the marketplace and collectively create a personal brand.

You need to commit to getting things done and invest the time in it. Alternatively, you can get an expert to help you get it done more quickly.

The five core components are:

1. **Value proposition.** We covered this in the previous chapter, but to recap briefly, you must be specific about who needs your expertise and what you are uniquely good at doing. This value proposition needs to come through clearly, whether you are communicating in person or on social-media platforms.

2. **Resume.** In a job search, this is your most important personal branding document as you will communicate your comprehensive value proposition through a headline, professional summary, experience, results and your education.

3. **LinkedIn profile.** This is the primary social platform for most people in mid to senior professional and management roles. You will find current and past colleagues, managers, partners and associates on LinkedIn, and they are all looking at the newsfeed and profiles. This presents a great opportunity to build a personal brand.

4. **STAR stories.** These help you to stand out when conversing with your target audience. They bring to life real challenges and the results you delivered to achieve a goal and are one of the most successful ways to become memorable once you meet with someone for an interview.

5. **Thought leadership articles.** Micro-publishing helps you share your ideas with your industry network, which is an immensely powerful way to educate others and build a following of engaged readers for whom you are top of mind.

Your value proposition, resume and STAR stories create a strong personal branding statement for one-to-one communication. Your LinkedIn profile and thought leadership articles create a strong personal branding statement for one-to-many communication.

Build a resume that stands out

In my career, I have reviewed over 20,000 resumes, as well as received feedback from senior managers in national and global corporations. I have had countless conversations giving advice on how to improve a resume. I have also delivered, with excitement, news that a candidate has secured an interview or job, as well as the crushing disappointment and the difficult conversation when a resume has been the reason why someone did not get invited to an interview.

This section is a definitive guide, based on my extensive experience, to creating a resume that will help you stand out, impress potential employers and secure interviews. Within larger organisations, it will help you move through the promotion process at higher speed and be front of the hiring manager's mind.

Your resume is a marketing document, a branding statement. It's a promise for the future, based on past accomplishments – a professional advertisement. It is written specifically for the purpose of motivating the targeted audience to contact you; it is **not** the complete guide to all your experiences, capabilities, education, interests and hobbies.

Think of a Porsche Cayenne. It has a glossy brochure as well as an owner's manual. The brochure has just enough information to make you want to head into the showroom, or at least fantasise about driving one. The owner's manual has all the information you need to operate every feature in the vehicle, but Porsche knows that it isn't going to motivate you to want to buy the car. So, let's agree that your resume is like a brochure – keep it brief, impressive and just enough to motivate people to want to interview you.

Your resume has financial value

Since your resume is the essential advertisement that will impress people and make them want to interview you, it has significant value in terms of its potential to open up opportunities and conversations for highly sought-after jobs with the best companies. To put a value on your resume, use this formula:

Current compensation x desired income growth (%) x years of income influenced = financial value of your resume.

Current compensation: this is the sum total of the base salary, incentives, bonuses and benefits in the job that you are in. If you are in between roles, it is your most recent employment agreement.

Desired income growth: this is the increase you need to keep up with your financial goals and lifestyle. For the sake of this example, let's say it will be 50% more than you are currently earning in two to three years from now – depending on how soon you want to get there. This number (1.5) will balance the lower amount you earned before and the higher amount you'll earn after the mid-point over a period of five years.

Years of income influenced: to keep within sight of the near term, it's best to use a period of the next five years. For example, if you are currently earning $200,000, the commercial value of your resume is worth $1.5 million ($200,000 x 1.5 x 5 years = $1.5 million). This is a high-value advertisement! Beyond money, it also affects your peace of mind, sense of accomplishment, enjoyment and satisfaction. And since your resume is a high-value advertisement, how much time are you going to spend on ensuring it inspires your buyers? I would hope it would be at least ten to twenty hours.

Your resume requires an investment of time

Unfortunately, most people I know don't spend more than an hour at best on their resume, and tend to work on updating it only when they have a moment or two to spare. As a result, they are not fully focused and have lower levels of energy, so end up with an average resume which doesn't inspire hiring managers or convert into interviews.

It's imperative to update your resume at a time when you have high energy and minimum distractions. I would even recommend taking a day off to get away to a secluded location and do deep thinking work on your all-important document, unless you get it done professionally.

People make a number of other mistakes along the way in relation to their resume. These include:

- Updating an older version of their resume

- Hastily adding a few lines

- Ignoring spelling and grammatical errors

- Forgetting critical success facts and figures

- Missing the opportunity to address the future direction they desire

This leads to:

- Formatting and grammatical errors that continue into the updated resume

- Information without persuasion

- Only the minimum required information

- Boring job description lines

- Lack of clarity about core value proposition and direction

Which leads to:

- Not being easily recognised in the ATS

- Not being shortlisted for jobs by junior HR screeners

- Not convincing recruiters to progress the application to the hiring managers

- Not inspiring hiring managers to imagine the applicant could be the answer to their needs

And finally, there is either silence or the standard rejection letter.

The long-term cost of these mistakes is significant. The effect of compounding mistakes and bad decisions adds up to a frustrating series of jobs and a sub-par career.

A resume must satisfy the five audiences in the hiring process

When applying for jobs online, there is a sequence of selection 'audiences' that your resume will pass through before it is presented to the real 'buyer' or decision maker – the hiring manager.

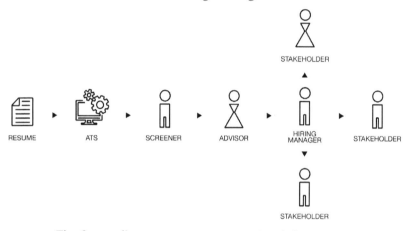

The five audiences your resume must satisfy

Audience #1: The ATS

Most major corporations in every industry use what's known as an applicant tracking system. The major ATS systems available – though they are often branded by the employer – include Workday, Taleo, SuccessFactors, Greenhouse and Jobvite, to name a few. Top companies receive thousands of applications and do not have the ability to read each resume, nor to shortlist applicants, so they use the ATS to score and rank resumes based on questions, keywords and increasingly complex AI algorithms.

Audience #2: The junior screener

The next selection audience is the junior HR or recruitment intern who is responsible for screening resumes and creating a shortlist. Again, due to lack of time in the workplace, role and industry, the job is given to someone who simply does not have the complex decision-making skills to look beyond titles and company names to determine whether there is a strong match or not. They are usually given a list of screening criteria that need to be compared to each resume before they pass it along to the next selection audience – the internal or external recruiter, or another level on to the hiring manager, depending on the size of the team.

Audience #3: The advisor – corporate recruitment/ HR or external recruitment

The third selection audience is usually the internal or external recruiter, occasionally the HR manager, who decides which candidates will be shortlisted for phone-based screening or interviews. They are often time-poor and have many internal 'customers' to please, as well as having metrics by which their performance and effectiveness are measured.

At this level, people will generally pick candidates based on the seven-second scroll to determine who looks the best and most relevant fit, predominantly based on the candidate's resume summary, titles, companies and maybe achievements in the last two jobs. Yep, all that in seven seconds! And if you resume catches their attention, then they will read it in detail.

These people are valued partners and key advisors in the recruitment process. They want to make sure they don't waste their time with unsuitable candidates who will make them look incompetent in front of the hiring manager.

Audience #4: The hiring manager

The next selection audience is the hiring manager. They are also time-poor, under pressure to drive results, have a demanding team to manage and targets to achieve. Often, they just don't have the time to interview seven to ten candidates and will depend on audiences #1–3 to deliver a quality shortlist of three to five candidates. They will give the top half of the first page of your resume 50% of their time, and then decide whether or not they will turn the page – so their decision is made on the top half of your first page.

Audience #5: The stakeholders

The last selection audience consists of the stakeholders. These are the people who will be impacted, either directly or indirectly, by a candidate's performance in the job. As such, they will be involved in the hiring process in one way or another.

Stakeholders include the manager's manager, team members, HR, indirect managers and anyone from other teams with whom the job needs to engage before, during or after the candidate's part in delivering results. The resume will be shared with them and they will form an opinion before the candidate even gets to meet them. When applying for a role, you therefore want to minimise room for negative comments and maximise positive comments.

A resume must align with the five hiring motives

Every job in an organisation exists for a purpose. A hiring motive is a driver and selection criterion in the interview process. The better your resume aligns with the motive, the more attractive it will look to those who review it.

The hiring motives are:

1. **Gain or profit**: how did you help your current or previous employer make money (eg you achieved sales targets, grew the customer base, developed new products etc)?

2. **Fear of loss**: how did you help your employer save money (eg you reduced costs, simplified customer-service processes, secured assets etc)?

3. **Satisfaction and comfort**: how did you make things better or easier for your employer (eg you ensured cultural fit, employee wellbeing and work-life balance etc)?

4. **Peace of mind**: how did you make things more secure for your employer (eg you engaged in service-level agreements, PR and operational excellence etc)?

5. **Pride and prestige**: how did you make the employer look good in the world (eg you hired from top universities and employers etc)?

Your resume must align with the relevant hiring motives for your job function. This the key factor for you to be invited to the interview process.

SWITCH TIP

Your resume must be a well-crafted marketing document which meets the needs of the five audiences and the five hiring motives.

Considering the fact that you have five audiences to satisfy and five hiring motives to fuel, it is essential you create a five-star resume. This will help each selection audience member to rank you among their top choices and create progressive velocity towards the hiring manager. It should also remove any possibility of them stopping or delaying your resume's progression towards the hiring manager.

Build a five-star resume

The five-star resume is a carefully designed document which communicates your value proposition in two to three pages. It must **satisfy the five audiences' selection criteria** and **meet the five hiring motives** for the job.

It needs to have these core components:

- Headline

- Professional summary (that supports your headline)

- Experience (that supports your summary)

- Results (that support your experience)

- Education (that supports your experience and results)

This is the architecture of 60% of professional resumes and is very common. What is less common is the **alignment** between each subsequent layer of this document.

When each component supports the one above, it creates an impressive document that helps the audience to reach a yes outcome. Just like the Eiffel Tower is aligned to stand out over the Parisian landscape, your resume needs to be aligned to stand out from the crowd – simple, yet impactful.

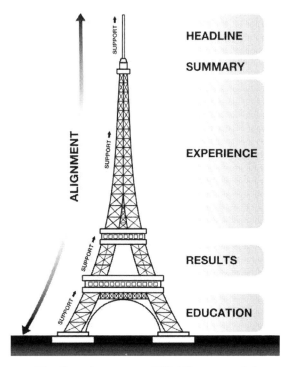

The five-star resume Eiffel Tower model

It's useful to point out what your resume is not. In all my time consulting to managers at global and national corporations, no one has been selected because of the fonts, colours or design enhancements on their resume. In fact, these can do more to harm than enhance your chances with the five selection audiences you're needing to communicate and align with.

The words you use to communicate your value proposition for employment in a role that you will be good at, will enjoy, and in which you will be well paid and can make a difference to the world are too precious to risk by trying to be overly innovative – unless you are a creative-industry professional showcasing your talent and design skills through your resume.

Please keep your resume simple in its style and layout, let the focus be on your words and what they say, and ensure you include the five core components.

1. Headline

This is the positioning statement about who you are, professionally. It should consist of two to five words, encapsulating the title you currently have or role you want to have, as well as the industry, unique keywords and, in the case of the second headline formula, a promise for results or past accomplishments.

Headline formula 1 = title/level + industry or distinct/ desirable keyword. For example:

- Sales leader – emerging technology

- Start-up sales leader in fintech

- General manager in wealth management

- B2B SaaS marketing manager

- Multinational human resources director

Headline formula 2 = title/level + industry or distinct/ desirable keyword + promise/accomplishment. For example:

- Rapid growth sales leader for emerging technology

- Innovative start-up sales leader in fintech | Keynote speaker

- Award-winning general manager in wealth management

- B2B SaaS marketing manager – digital marketing pioneer

- Multinational human resources director | author of *Culture Eats Strategy for Breakfast*

2. Summary

This is your sixty-second elevator pitch – your value proposition. It's the movie trailer; your opportunity to show the recruiter the highlights of your skills, experiences and results. Ensure that this expands, aligns with and supports your headline, and write it with the next role you will desire in mind to ensure it aligns with your future direction as well.

Summary formula = desired and recent title/s, reputable employers, skills/capabilities, results and recognition. For example:

Jason Bourne is a sales director with rapid growth software companies in emerging technologies like Microsoft, ServiceNow and Blue Prism. Winner of Sales Leader of the

Year 202X and President's Club in 20XX, 20XX and 20XX. Track record of increasing top-line sales by 30–50% annually, penetrating major accounts and securing lighthouse customers. Developed proven methodology for attracting top talent, building a high-performance culture and achieving ambitious growth plans.

3. Experience

Hiring managers for companies employ people they are like and those they want to be like – this is the baseline. As well as a good cultural and experiential fit, they want people to be an aspirational fit, so it doesn't matter if you have come from a smaller or larger company, as long as there is something that is aspirational in your experience.

People working at startups and fast-growing companies can highlight being action-oriented, agile with opportunity and having the ability to make a big difference in a short amount of time. People working at larger organisations can highlight getting results at scale, driving complex high-value engagements and delivering strategic transformational outcomes.

Keep your experience to a brief sentence because most people only read about the company and role, then assume what your responsibilities are. The formula you can use in creating your resume experience is:

Experience formula = companies, role and brief description of responsibility (reports, territory, targets, products and industry). For example:

- Company: Microsoft <Location> Jan 20XX–current

- Title: sales director

- Led the new and emerging business unit, consisting of seven direct reports, providing solutions across IOT, HoloLens and AI technologies, delivering transformational outcomes to the financial services industry and on an annual target of $10 million

4. Results

This is the most important and impactful set of words you will communicate about yourself. Your job description is the minor and your results are the major. Your results enable the hiring manager to imagine what you could accomplish in the future working at their company, based on your past performance.

This is where you need to spend 70% of your time and energy, digging deep into your memory to capture, refine and quantify the results you have achieved. You will use this section to list awards and recognition, ie formal or social proof of performance. Never have I had a hiring manager complain that a candidate's resume had 'too many numbers'.

You will need to use success verbs (positive accomplishment words) to present the results you achieved. Every line in your resume should have metrics ($,% etc) to demonstrate the results you achieved. No matter how much you think is enough, you can always add some more quantification. Results presented with success verbs and quantification directly address the five motives and audiences.

Results formula = success verb, hiring motive and result quantification.

Examples:

- Achieved 122% of annual quota/target for 20XX

- Increased public cloud revenue by 150%

- Acquired twenty-two new clients from the financial services industry

- Introduced four sales campaigns, yielding $4.5 million in net new revenue

- Reduced average sales cycle from thirteen months to nine months

- Expanded solution footprint in top ten major accounts by 62%

- Secured five global case studies from key customers

- Improved sales culture with increased managerial effectiveness rating from 3.7 to 4.6 (out of 5)

- Awarded Sales Leader of the Year 20XX at annual conference

- Selected for Microsoft's 'high potential program' for accelerating managers into senior leadership

Other success verbs you could use include accelerated, contributed, decreased, delivered, exceeded, generated, gained, grew, improved, produced and saved.

5. Education, certifications and professional interests

Your education can be a supportive foundation if it helps your future career direction. For example, an MBA from a prestigious school will be well regarded for a management role in most major organisations. On the other hand, a Bachelor of Science in Zoology, for example, completed in the late eighties or early nineties means very little because that education does not support your current profession. But it still demonstrates that you pursued further education and completed what you started.

If you had a minor subject in Economics, that might be worthwhile mentioning to align with and support your current position today. It's useful to note any professional development or certifications you've completed in the last ten years in this section, along with certifications that have helped you to become a better leader for your team, or a thought leader for your industry and customers. These can include leadership development programs, a coaching certification, sales training and industry-specific training.

You can also use this section to add keywords by which you would like to be found by the five selection audiences. Alternatively, you could add these keywords in a separate section called 'Professional interests', or another option is to intersperse them throughout your resume. Keywords could include topics and areas you already know, as well as those that interest you. They can be helpful with ranking and getting you found in ATS-driven hiring and LinkedIn searches.

The examples you can use in creating this section are:

Education:

- <University Name> 2018–2020. Master of Business Administration

- <University Name> 1992–1996. Bachelor of Arts – Economics Major

Certifications and professional development:

- High Potential Leadership Development 2020

- Target Account Selling 2018

- Challenger Selling 2017

- Peak Performance Coaching 2016

Professional interests:

- Digital transformation programs, AI, machine learning (ML), cloud automation and orchestration, Internet of Things (IOT), virtual reality (VR), HoloLens, public cloud, hybrid cloud, cloud services, managed services, serverless computing, nanotechnology, biotechnology, cognitive science, robotic process automation (RPA) and psychotechnology.

In summary, your resume can be one among a thousand 'buildings', or it can be like the Eiffel Tower, standing out and memorable. A five-star resume has a clear visual hierarchy matching the mental model of the reader. A simple, flowing structure makes it easier for them to absorb essential information. It tells a compelling story about your career.

Ensure you use easy-to-read fonts with headlines in bold (section, company and titles) and white spaces between sections and jobs. Use short sentences (long sentences will not be read and will lose impact). You are giving recruiters a quick burst of information that needs to be enough for them to say yes and contact you for an interview.

Find the five-star resume template and how to avoid the top fifteen mistakes people make when writing their resume at www.switch.work/bonus.

Build your five-star LinkedIn profile

In a matter of seconds, your LinkedIn profile is within reach of anyone in the world, so make sure it looks great because it will be judged. As soon as your name is mentioned by a friend, employee or recruiter as a potential candidate, it is highly likely that the hiring manager will instantly search for you on LinkedIn. What they see on your profile has the power to start or stop a potential interview process in its tracks. As such, it is essential that your LinkedIn profile is the best representation of you and your personal branding.

There are five levels of LinkedIn profile strength, based on the information you have (or haven't) completed:

- Beginner (<50% complete)

- Intermediate (50%)

- Advanced (75%)

- Expert (90%)

- All-Star (100%)

The All-Star profile is the top tier of rating for profile completion you can receive from LinkedIn. Your profile must have seven elements to qualify for an All-Star rating:

- Profile photo

- Up-to-date current position (with a description)

- Two past positions

- Education

- Skills (a minimum of three)

- Industry and location

- Fifty or more connections

A complete profile is the starting point, but we are going to take this much further and create a five-star LinkedIn profile to meet the needs of the five audiences and five hiring motives. It goes beyond informing, to influencing your audience.

Ten steps to building your five-star LinkedIn profile

Using ten steps (as well as implementing the concepts I outlined in the five-star resume section), build your strong personal branding statement on LinkedIn.

1. Profile photo

If a picture speaks a thousand words, make sure it tells a great story. In terms of your attire, a good rule is to think about how your employer would like you to come across to their clients. Suiting up, smart casual or dressing down is a matter of matching your audience, or perhaps go one step up. Don't use last week's photo of you at a friend's barbecue (believe me, I have seen a few), but include an acceptable headshot with a neutral background (such as a white wall). Have it taken in daylight using a good camera or the latest phone. You can get a professional headshot done, which will take your photo to a whole new level.

2. Background image

Everything about your profile, including your background image, says something about you. It's your personal brand. You can choose from a few stock photo options available from LinkedIn, upload an image of your choice or design a custom background on www. canva.com. Ensure that it's not too busy to distract attention from your face, but a great supplementary background can enhance the look and feel of your profile, and in so doing, send out the right message.

3. Headline

Refer to the PVP section in Chapter Six.

4. About

Refer to the resume summary section in this chapter.

5. Articles and activity

This section is the key differentiator between using LinkedIn as a resume or as a personal branding platform to increase your influence. Sharing your insight about an area in which you have expertise, and contributing your ideas to a conversation/s within that domain, sets you apart as an influencer. You can find out more about this in the last section of this chapter on building your influence through writing and publishing thought leadership articles.

6. Experience

Use the guidelines we covered earlier in this chapter to build your five-star resume and create high-impact sentences using success verbs, hiring motives and result quantification. You can choose to do this in three ways:

1. Job success content written for future employers

2. Job success content written for clients

3. Job success content written for clients and future employers

The key to deciding which way to do this is figuring out which of your two audiences are on LinkedIn and which one impacts your career success in a near to mid-term timeframe. Whatever your answer is, you are right, so write your content accordingly. I strongly recommend short sentences in bullet points, given that people tune out with lengthy sentences and bloated text. You can choose to:

1. Remove quantification (although this is a powerful way to differentiate yourself)

2. Remove client names. For example, you could say, 'Led $10 million win for digital transformation at a major bank/financial services company'

You can also showcase your experience by adding rich media. LinkedIn will let you add photos, sites, videos, presentations and documents. This is a great place to add a photo of yourself receiving an award, speaking at an event, displaying formal recognition or even completing a marathon – anything that demonstrates the desirable characteristics of resilience and accomplishment.

7. Education, licences and certifications

Include your university and postgraduate education. If you have a number of degrees and educational qualifications which support the job you are in and the one you would like to pursue next, please ensure you update your qualifications here. That being said, if your qualifications are getting beyond five years old, I recommend adding only those that are most relevant and beneficial to your future employer and build credibility in your job.

8. Skills

I recommend choosing five to ten skills which are also keywords that describe components of what you do or the industry you work in. LinkedIn doesn't only show viewers people who are mutual connections, it also shows those who are highly skilled in something because they have a good number of skill endorsements. This builds trust and credibility.

9. Recommendations

This is another great feature that sets LinkedIn apart from a resume. Getting a written endorsement from people builds your credibility and trust with the reader. Increasingly as a society, we depend on other people's ratings about products (Google), restaurants (Yelp) and hotels (TripAdvisor), so why not for professional competence and performance?

Keep in mind, the more senior the title of the endorsee, the more impressive the recommendation will be. A CEO endorsement is the best, followed by a vice president, then director, and so on. Avoid reciprocal endorsements, where you write an endorsement for your endorsees because it seems to be a mutually beneficial exchange. This reduces the impact of the endorsement.

10. Accomplishments

Choose your top five to seven professional accomplishments and list them here. This helps you stand out as an accomplished manager, and you can also add honours/awards you've received, publications, projects, organisations and more.

It is possible to get your LinkedIn profile to an All-Star status in just a few hours. I recommend you go on to build a five-star profile, keeping the five audiences and motives in mind at all times. And who knows what opportunities this might bring in the future?

I also recommend checking your other social-media channels if you use them (like Facebook, Twitter, Instagram etc). See if there is any content that could be seen as undesirable. You then have three options available to you:

1. Change your profile setting to private so only your friends/followers/connections can see it

2. Remove photos or content that could be considered inappropriate by your target audience

3. Adopt a 'take it or leave it' approach, because your social footprint will be found and it will be judged

---

MR PINK PUBES'S STORY: KNOW YOUR AUDIENCE

A few years back, I introduced a relationship manager to a market-leading global corporation for a role which focused on managing the company's relationship in the Government and Defence agencies. All was going well, until his Twitter profile picture was discovered. In it, he was at the beach with a generous pink feather strategically placed to cover his crotch – and he was wearing nothing else!

I called and discussed this with him, but he couldn't see why conservative politicians, generals and bureaucrats would have a problem with it. That's where the dialogue ended as the company couldn't have Mr Pink Pubes as the face of its brand to its largest clients.

You either align with your audience or you change to another audience which you align with better.

Be the STAR of the interview with storytelling

When I debrief clients after they have met with a candidate, I ask them, 'What stood out most to you about <candidate's name>?', and 70% of the time, they say, 'It was the story they shared about...' People love stories. We've grown up with them and we give Hollywood billions of dollars by watching the stories it tells in movies. Stories capture our attention; they stir our emotions. We believe stories and we remember them. So go ahead and tell the person interviewing you stories about situations where you have:

1. Solved the problems they and their company are facing

2. Achieved results that they are seeking

3. Demonstrated the character, skill and experience they are desiring

If you aren't sure how to do this, then let me introduce you to the STAR model. The acronym STAR stands for:

- **S**ituation
- **T**ension
- **A**ction
- **R**esult

It's a simple-to-remember and easy-to-deliver model for telling your stories.

S – Situation

The first step of this model is where you describe a relevant situation from before it became a problem until it was at its peak. Mention the key people, places and components that were contributing to or impacted by the situation. Most importantly, communicate why this was a problem, what could have happened if it hadn't been solved and by when it had to be solved (if there was a timeframe involved).

T – Tension

The second step is where you describe the build-up, the series of unfortunate events and challenges that the situation would have created for others if it had not been resolved – the people, processes, places, economic impact etc. What was the tension? What was the severity of the issue? Use appropriate emotion to share how you felt about it, what you thought about it and why you decided to act.

A - Action

The third step is to describe what you did about the issue. How did you take the initiative to solve the problem? Whom did you involve? What was the method you used to steer the situation around/over/through the obstacles to achieve the result you desired? Structure this information in three to five steps maximum.

This needs to be about you and is your moment to shine – so take it.

Acknowledge the team, but keep the focus on your action/s. After all, the team involved isn't interviewing for your ideal role – you are. The prospective employer is not hiring the team that supported you, they are hiring you, so talk about what you did.

R - Result

The final step in this model is to talk about the results. What was the new situation when the issue had been resolved? What was the evidence of success? What did people say? How did this impact the team, the company, the customers and partners? Use appropriate emotion to share this. What did you learn from it? How did this experience change you? What have you taken from this experience? How has it prepared you for this moment?

SWITCH TIP

Your stories make you memorable, believable and influential.

Your STAR story does not have to be a ten-minute presentation (although it could be). My advice is to tailor the same STAR story in varying levels of detail for these communication channels:

- Phone call: a one- to two-minute version of the story

- In-person conversation: a two- to five-minute version

- One-to-many presentation: a ten-minute version of the story

You can communicate your STAR story through a variety of formats:

- In person (at meetings and presentations)

- Audio (on the phone, via podcasts and recorded expert interviews)

- Video (via authority videos and testimonials)

- Documents (via social posts, infographics and case studies)

The biggest mistake people make is not to prepare the stories they are going to share before they meet the hiring manager. As a result, the story lacks the full detail and potential.

You can write a STAR story in a one-page document and email it to the hiring manager after the interview as a means of building a relationship, staying top of mind and becoming a stand-out candidate in their process. This creates influence and a means to address questions that you may not have answered to your best ability in the interview or may have run out of time to discuss. If you make your story about solving their problems and achieving their results, you will always have their attention.

You can find more about being the STAR of the interview with storytelling at www.switch.work/bonus.

Write and publish thought leadership articles

LinkedIn states:

> 'We're always looking for new ways for members to contribute professional insights on LinkedIn. Our publishing platform allows members, in addition to Influencers, to publish articles about their expertise and interests.'

How do you want to be perceived in the industry in which you are likely to spend the rest of your working career – as significant or insignificant? You choose.

You can write and publish articles that cover:

1. Stories about your experiences and learnings from the past that will benefit others

2. Observations about current events and news

3. Predictions and trends for the future

4. Anything that will interest you or your target audience

5. Solutions and breakthroughs your company's products are providing

This content is showcased in your professional LinkedIn profile. It can be found prominently in the Articles section. The articles get shared with your connections and their followers. LinkedIn sometimes sends out notifications, and if it's a popular article, it will be included in Trending Articles.

You might believe there are those much smarter than you who could say something better about your chosen subjects, but more than ever before, people are looking to learn from their peers' real experience. They want authentic, raw stories rather than perfectly packaged bites of information. You are uniquely qualified to share your views about something that is relevant to your job or industry **through the lens of your life, work and experience.**

How I got approached by *Business Insider*

I started writing articles on LinkedIn a while back. These included topics that were relevant to the target audience I wanted to educate, serve and engage. Here is a sample list of my article topics, sorted by the number of views:

- 'How To Manage Difficult But Top-Performing Team Members': 308 views

- 'How To Manage Unrealistic Expectations Of Senior Management': 528 views

- '10 REAL Reasons Why Top Sales Performers Will Leave Your Team': 959 views

- 'Five Steps To A Successful Performance Improvement Plan': 1,922 views

- 'How To Attract Top Sales Performers To Your Company': 2,611 views

- 'How To Manage Managers: Six Best Practices': 4,924 views

- 'Six Career Benefits Of Being Open To Talking To A Recruiter': 11,245 views

Each of these views included not only my Level 1 connections, but Level 2, 3 and other connections. The subset of likes, comments and direct messages to my inbox was encouraging and helped me gain the attention of my target audience. This was the case until I wrote 'Five Things Only Bad Bosses Say'. That got... wait for it... drumroll... 176,893 views!

Until that point, my highest viewer/readership had been 11,245, and that itself was more than I'd ever expected, but a 15x increase in views was extraordinary! And what followed was even more interesting.

1. I was featured in the 'Recently Posted' section of 'Leadership & Management' along with Richard Branson and Jack Welch.

2. After a few days, the editor of *Business Insider* messaged me and asked for permission to repost the article on their site.

3. This led to those at *Business Insider* saying they loved the content and style, and asking for more articles.

4. Which helped me pitch the idea of posting my content to my contacts at HubSpot, whose blog is the most read sales and marketing blog in the United States.

The benefits of publishing thought leadership articles

As a result of writing, posting and publishing the thought leadership articles I created, I have received benefits that have yielded great advantages to my career and influence:

1. I stand out in a noisy, competitive industry for my expertise because I create content that shows my experience and insight.

2. My content has a viewership among my audience, which increases visibility, trust and a desire to work with me.

3. I have been able to build relationships with people who don't know me, one-on-one and one-to-many, when I mention the articles, and follow up with reference to these by sending links via email.

4. People can refer me to others with confidence because they have direct exposure to my expertise.

5. The media have approached me looking for great content to share, which strengthens my positioning as a (micro) influencer in my industry, and deeming my content worthy of posting to their audience. This is useful to mention to prospective clients because not too many recruiters get published by *Business Insider*.

Writing articles can be time consuming and challenging if you're not sure what to say and wonder whether your content is good enough. I have the same issues. At times I have gone six to eight months between writing articles, and at other times I've been able to write more often. And yet, once it's done, it remains out there forever. It may not be easy, but it is possible.

I like to write an article, sleep on it, pivot quickly and revise, then get it out there. Personally, I live by the premise that done is better than perfect. And so can you.

SWITCH ACTION

Having completed this chapter, write down at least one thing you've learned and one action you need to take. You may like to use the Switch actions sheet at www.switch.work/bonus to record your learning points and action plan.

EIGHT

Engage Your Network To Build Your Net Worth

Switch from being a stranger to a friend.

The age of influencers

You don't have to go too far to see a twenty-two-year-old influencer making millions off their YouTube channel, or a fifteen-year-old streaming their gameplay on Twitch and making far more money than their parents' income combined. This is the age of influencers, and their followers who enable these people to monetise that influence. And we aren't talking about a million subscribers either – companies nowadays are seeking micro-influencers with at least 1,000 engaged followers who are consuming the content they create.

Your social capital and influence come from your network. People will always prefer those they know and trust over those they don't know. In the context of careers, it is essential that you are known in your industry. It is no secret that those who are seen as the go-to people in an industry will be the ones to be first informed about great career opportunities and, in fact, be pursued with hard-to-refuse offers.

Networking is about building and maintaining relationships for future mutual benefit. It happens passively by getting to know people as you progress through the seasons of life. It is done in person as well as online, but the ROI for networking online (one-to-many) does beat in-person networking (one to one) any day. That said, it is best to use both approaches to connect and stay in touch.

LinkedIn influencer

LinkedIn has helped us identify, connect and communicate with classmates, colleagues, partners and industry contacts like never before. I'm interested to see an update from someone who has won an award, is celebrating a milestone or announcing they are hiring when I wasn't even aware they had changed jobs.

LinkedIn has a built-in client and employer audience all in the one place. This is networking nirvana, so I am going to focus in this chapter on using LinkedIn to build influence in your network as you grow, engage and essentially build a community of like-minded people who collaborate to advance each other's careers and lives.

Take a look at LinkedIn's definition of what an Influencer is and does.

LinkedIn's Influencers are selected by the social media giant on an invitation-only basis. They comprise a global collective of 500 of the world's most influential thinkers, innovators and leaders. LinkedIn's editors work with these thought leaders, such as Bill Gates, Ariana Huffington and Mary Barra, to create content which the company hopes will help their members become more informed and 'spark thoughtful conversations'.

Influence is not exclusively reserved for CEOs. It exists at every level in an organisation and industry. You may not be Richard Branson or Bill Gates with LinkedIn's team interviewing you, but you have the same option available to you – to post and share content. This is an incredible opportunity for you to step up and stand out in a noisy and competitive industry.

The LinkedIn Social Selling Index (SSI)

LinkedIn's Social Selling Index is an invaluable tool to measure how effective you are in:

1. Establishing your professional brand. When you complete your LinkedIn profile, do so with your ideal employer in mind. Publish meaningful posts and become a thought leader.

2. Finding the right people. Via the use of LinkedIn's search function, you can identify your ideal employers.

3. Engaging with insights. When you discover and share what LinkedIn terms 'conversation-worthy' updates, you will be far more likely to create and grow relationships.

4. Building relationships. Establish trust with decision makers to strengthen your network.

You can find your Social Selling Index rank at www.linkedin.com/sales/ssi and as you build your community, engage your audience and create interesting content, LinkedIn might even invite you to become a LinkedIn Influencer.

SWITCH TIP

A great LinkedIn profile along with consistent posts, articles, comments, status updates and shares will build your influence.

How to build your influence on LinkedIn

Start taking these steps today to become a micro-influencer.

1. Connect with everyone you know, meet and have a positive or neutral relationship with

This includes classmates, former colleagues, managers, people in other teams, current colleagues, partners, clients and others you have worked with outside of your current capacity. I recommend including friends and family members who are in the corporate world. As you meet new people, add them on a weekly basis. You cannot overestimate how many times somebody has benefited because of a friend-of-a-friend.

2. Join groups that are relevant and will benefit your career

This is a great way to stay up to date with industry trends, notice key individuals within your industry and start a conversation on a trending topic in the groups. Increasingly, people who interact on social networks with other people they have never met, feel like they 'know' them. People are open and receptive to communicating online with members of a group they have not met before, with a greater degree of trust and openness than if they'd met those people on the street and discussed the same topics.

Participating in groups helps showcase your experience and build relationships, and you can follow up with connections to members who are of interest and relevant to you. This can then lead to in-person meetings and opportunities to work together and help each other along in your career journeys.

3. Be visible (or be forgotten)

This means creating great content like status updates, articles, photos and videos that will be of interest and help to your audience. In addition, comment on other people's posts and share them, celebrate wins, message your connections about something interesting or beneficial, or ask for their input by mentioning them on a post. You could go further and seek opportunities to speak at events, get on a video and get PR coverage. Success comes from modelling other successful people, but more than that, engagement creates familiarity. And familiarity builds trust.

4. Always be helping

People are focused on achieving their goals and solving their problems. Most topics that could benefit you are likely to be of interest to you, too. This is the same with the people you connect with, so always be looking for ways to help people. People are conditioned to return a favour, so the more you help people, the more likely they are to help you when you need it.

5. Follow companies that interest you and connect with key people of interest

This keeps you up to date, and you can go a step further and proactively connect with your future target hiring managers or talent acquisition/internal recruitment department within the organisation. This helps them notice you, as well as the content you are sharing and the connections you have in common. Collectively, they move from being a stranger to becoming familiar over a period of time. You don't have to work with them immediately, but building a relationship and being visible is beneficial to you, and to them because you could always refer people and other opportunities that may interest them.

6. Embrace your personal brand building as personal development

Finding the creativity, courage and commitment to share insights and help others is a journey in personal development. It's likely that you could simply be far too busy to do all of this – it can seem like a lot of work. In some ways, you would be right, and in other ways, you are not.

This is far more about quality and consistency than quantity and time. I recommend spending fifteen minutes each day on LinkedIn with the purpose of building engagement with your network. You can do this during a morning or evening commute or a break in the middle of the day. In this way, you'll get far more done in a week than if you were to sit down for a full hour or more to do it all at once.

I also recommend writing at least one article each month if you are passively building your personal brand. If you are actively building it and looking to change roles soon, post an article once a week.

7. Aim for an engaged community of collaborative people

Becoming an influencer is about building authentic, meaningful connections with people online and in person, which will benefit as many people as possible. This opens the doors of opportunity beyond job change to career acceleration. The sharing of information, insights, opportunities and collaborative partnerships will create the best circumstances for you to continue enjoying success in the future. We are better together.

Find more information on how to build your influence on LinkedIn at www.switch.work/bonus.

SWITCH ACTION

Having completed this chapter, write down at least one thing you've learned and one action you need to take. You may like to use the Switch actions sheet at www.switch.work/bonus to record your learning points and action plan.

SECTION FOUR
JOB TARGET

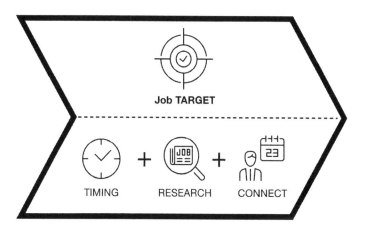

Job TARGET

TIMING + RESEARCH + CONNECT

NINE

The Right Timing Creates The Right Results

PRINCIPLE

Switch from too late to right on time.

Imagine it's 2pm at work. You've had a busy day. You haven't eaten and you are hungry. You step out of the office building and walk to the food court. Everything looks and smells great right now. You make a quick decision, buy something unhealthy and eat it.

Then regret strikes. You ask yourself, 'Why did I eat that? It looked good at the time, but I know I shouldn't have.' Now you're doing the walk of shame back to the office.

Some people treat their careers like this. They are busy with work, ignoring the signs that they badly need some self-care, and then when things get bad, they rush out to find the next job – and often regret it. You might be one of them. You work hard, stay busy – busy, busy, busy – and don't notice opportunities that could improve your current job and accelerate your career towards your goals.

Then, something changes. A new manager you can't stand joins the team, the company announces job cuts, you miss targets and the pressure mounts. Now you realise you need to find another job, and quickly, so you look at online jobs, apply for a few, go to a couple of interviews and accept the best available one, only to regret it three to six months down the track. But unlike the food court analogy, where you can make different food choices each day, you can't do this when it comes to your job and career. You don't get to choose a different job to work in every day, so don't treat your employment like your lunchtime choices.

Timing of changing jobs

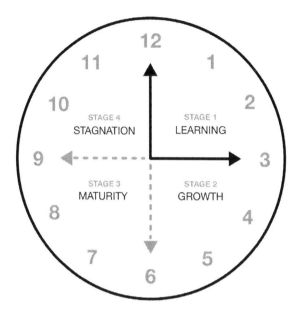

Job maturity clock

Given that timing and objectivity are critical in the process of finding and changing jobs and a career, I'm often asked, 'When is a good time to start looking for a new job?'

I say, 'It depends what time it is on your job maturity clock.'

Consider a classic analogue watch or clock with a long hour hand and a shorter minute hand. If we go in a clockwise direction around the watch or clock face, we follow the phases of how your learning, results and satisfaction in your job will typically track over time.

Stages of the job maturity clock

Stage one: the learning phase. This stage is typically your first two to three months in a new job. It is the phase of *high learning and low results.*

Stage two: the growth phase. This stage will typically range from six to eighteen months. During this stage, you are gaining knowledge and understanding of your environment and analysing its strengths, weaknesses, opportunities and threats (SWOT). You have settled into your job and are achieving results. Your productivity and results keep improving. This is the phase of *high learning and high results.*

Stage three: the maturity phase. This stage can typically range from one to three years. It is the time when you're achieving your peak performance in the role. You know your environment well. You are highly productive and making a difference in your job. This is the phase of *low learning and high results.*

Stage four: the stagnation phase. This stage can come as early as eighteen months or up to three years, depending on your career trajectory, the speed of change in your role and the company and industry. In this phase there is little or no learning and personal development, so you are no longer growing in the role and you can do your job 'with your eyes closed'. This is the phase of *low learning and diminishing or low results.*

Sometimes your results remain high, but the expectations of performance have gone even higher. In the words of a number of high achievers, 'I have become a victim of my own success'.

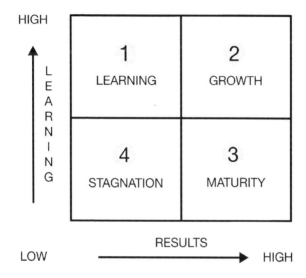

Job maturity stages

SWITCH TIP

Don't be reactive, but rather, be proactive when it comes to changing jobs. You want to be able to balance rationale with emotion and make the best decision that is a fit with your values and career goals.

Job maturity learning and results

I recommend to people that the learning and growth phases are too early to look to change jobs. You really need to get to the maturity phase and achieve results to even be open to exploring opportunities. This stage has a good give-get ratio, where you have received investment of time, energy and resources from your company, and you are giving back results and making a difference.

SWITCH TIP

The best job and career moves are made in the maturity phase, when you've been in your role for two to three years.

It's in the maturity and stagnation phases – the second half of your time in the role – that you need to switch on to opportunities within and outside your organisation, and be ready to explore and assess each opportunity on its merit and fit with your values and goals. Like professional athletes who move between clubs, timing is critical to maximising your value.

SWITCH ACTION

Having completed this chapter, write down at least one thing you've learned and one action you need to take. You may like to use the Switch actions sheet at www.switch.work/bonus to record your learning points and action plan.

TEN

Research Your Audience Like A Pro

PRINCIPLE

Switch from a lack of awareness to being well-informed.

It is critical to research your target jobs, people and companies to be able to connect and secure interviews with them. When companies hire, they struggle to find the right people quickly. That's why a multi-billion-dollar recruitment industry exists to solve this problem. So, when you are looking, ensure that you make the people at companies and jobs you are interested in aware that you are looking as soon as possible. They will welcome the interest of a relevant and well-presented potential candidate. It's a win-win.

A good list of companies and contacts to reach out to can make a big difference in how soon you start talking to potential employers. When you have a number of different job opportunities in consideration at the same time, you can be choosy about what is important to you and say no to jobs that aren't a good fit for your career aspirations.

Research companies

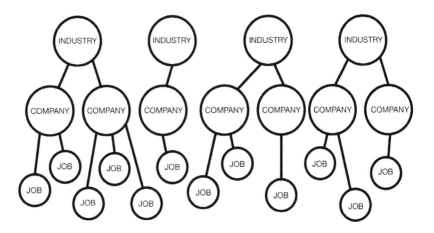

There are two proactive approaches you can take to targeting what you want in terms of a new job. Applying either one, you will position yourself ahead of others. You can see a visual representation of these two approaches in the image:

Top-down approach. You decide the industries that you want to target, identify the key companies within them and the relevant jobs within those companies.

Bottom-up approach. You decide on the jobs that you want to target, identify the key companies that offer these roles, and then research the industries these companies are in.

Once you have decided on the industry, companies and job/s that you are going to pursue, it's time to position yourself and focus on the key people you need to contact during this process. Google is your first and best point of reference to start researching companies, but these additional sources can assist you in locating useful company insights:

- Annual reports

- Wikipedia

- Glassdoor – current and past employees

- Company social-media pages – LinkedIn, YouTube, Facebook, Twitter

- Google News

- Industry analysts

Research key people

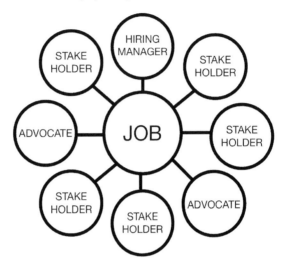

Hiring managers are the people you will report to. They are responsible for delivering results, and you will make a critical contribution to their success or failure. This is the most important relationship in the key people cast as hiring managers coach and lead you to peak performance and productivity. They are the most motivated to find a replacement or potential future hire because they are always under pressure to deliver results.

Stakeholders are the people who are invested in the hiring process and impacted by your performance in the job. They include your manager's manager, colleagues, HR, corporate recruiters, indirect managers and anyone from other teams whom the job needs to engage with before, during or after your part in delivering results.

Advocates are the people who know you in your target organisation and will have an influence on the hiring process. They are stakeholders who can be an internal supporter for you, recommend you to others and register you as a referral for jobs. They are highly valuable in the interview process as they can provide you with information about the organisation's culture, vision, strategy, people, challenges and opportunities. This can equip and enable you to make a fully informed decision and succeed in the process.

Informers are people you know in the target organisation or those who have a strong relationship with someone in the target organisation (spouse, sibling or close friend). They are not stakeholders so they can't be an advocate for you internally because they may not know the hiring manager and key stakeholders well enough or have influence with them, but they genuinely want to support you and can do so with information about the organisation's culture, vision, strategy, people, challenges and opportunities.

SWITCH TIP

There are a number of people who surround each job. Understanding the key people enables you to prepare to influence them.

Advisors are the people who do not have a vested interest in the organisation. They are not stakeholders; they are your coaches, counsellors, friends and loved ones. These include mentors, past colleagues, industry experts, others at your level and those ahead of you too. This board of advisors has your best interests at heart and can be objective about the job. You can take facts, thoughts and feelings to them, and they will give you their opinions about whether the job is right for you or not.

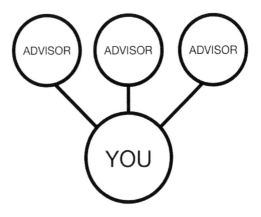

Create a target list of contacts

This list needs to include the company, job and key people to contact in your search. It will be a dynamic list that needs updating and will be your key point of reference in implementing your job change strategy.

Here is an example of a list you can create with your target contacts based on industry, company, job details and contact information:

Contact's company, name and title. You will need this to know whom to contact in the company.

Category. You need to know the role they will play in the process (eg hiring manager, stakeholder, advocate or supporter).

Contact's email and phone/mobile number. You will need this to be able to reach people based on your preferred method of contact.

Contact's LinkedIn profile. This is the single best source of information available about people. You will learn their industry, company, name, title and job details on LinkedIn. If you are connected, you may also be able to see their email and phone number in the contact section.

Status of contacts. This is for you to keep track of what action you have taken so far and to sort your list based on these categories:

- Yet to contact/not contacted

- Contacted, no reply (to be followed up)

- Contacted/in conversations (from initial discussions to interview process completion)

- Contacted and completed conversations

Notes. This is where you can update information based on the progression of conversations with the person/people. Notes include details they have provided, next action/s to be taken, and by whom.

SWITCH TIP

LinkedIn has changed the game for careers, so start with LinkedIn as your first point of information gathering about people.

Using LinkedIn to research people

Searching on LinkedIn:

- If you know the name of the person you wish to contact, enter it in the search box and select the person's profile.

- If you are looking for a title but don't know the person's name, try company name, title and city in your search. The more unique details you use about a person in the search query, the more likely you are to find them.

- If you aren't able to find the person through a search on LinkedIn, try doing a search on Google by their name, company, title and city.

Purchasing a LinkedIn subscription:

- Purchase a Sales Navigator subscription. I recommend this over a LinkedIn Premium Career subscription because of the incredible company and contact targeting abilities. This will help you conduct searches with ease to locate key contacts in your target companies, which is worth the subscription alone. At the time of writing, LinkedIn states you can cancel at any time.

Categorising key people:

- As you browse through people's profiles, I recommend categorising them based on their titles with reference to the role/s into which they fit (eg hiring managers, stakeholders, advocates and advisors).

- For each contact you want to connect with, take a look at the full list of mutual connections you have (this is my favourite feature). Invite them to connect on LinkedIn, and in your connection request, mention contacts you have in common. You could also call or message the people you have in common and ask for more information about your target contact – perhaps an introduction or an endorsement, or maybe they could refer you at that company for a job.

- If your common contact is not willing to do this for you, they are not an advocate for you or the manager you wish to contact or the role – it's better to figure this out before you drop their name in conversation. I have seen instances where people have mentioned a name in common, and either the target contact didn't like that person or the person in common didn't support the candidate.

- You know you have an advocate when they will make introductions for you, refer you to jobs and other stakeholders, and support you through the hiring process downstream.

Finding email addresses:

- In LinkedIn, you can see the contact info for your Level 1 connections. You can also message them on LinkedIn. If the person you want to contact is not a current connection, I'd recommend sending an invitation to connect.

- If you aren't connected to the person, you could figure out their work email address with a good chance of success. Mid to large companies tend to use a predictable email naming system like firstname.lastname@companydomainname. Smaller companies will often follow slight variations on their email naming system, like firstname@companydomainname or firstnamefirstletterlastname@companydomainname.

- For more advanced search methods, you can use tools like VoilaNorbert, Hunter and MailTester which identify common email patterns. Some also offer Chrome plugins with on-page information scourers.

Finding phone numbers:

- You can easily look at a company website to find your potential contact's board number. If you'd prefer to find a mobile/cell phone number of a person at the company, you could connect with them on LinkedIn (see previous note about contact info).

- If this doesn't work, you could message someone you know that you have in common and with whom you have a good relationship and ask for a favour. You could say something like, 'Hi *<name of your contact>*, I noticed that you are connected on LinkedIn to *<name of mutual contact>*. I need to reach him/her and was hoping you could help me. You can usually see their email and phone number in contact info just under their profile if you are connected to them. Can you check and send this to me please? It would be really helpful. Thanks.'

- If you don't have someone you know in common, there are a number of subscription-based tools which provide you with B2B information. This is a dynamic space and there are often tools appearing while others disappear.

- Some people may frown upon contacting others by phone or email when it is unsolicited. You could allow this to be an obstacle or you could overcome it, but you've got to do what you've got to do if it is the only thing standing between you and a meaningful conversation that could benefit both you and the other person.

Once you have your target contact profile/s in front of you, prepare to connect with these people.

Set up job alerts on LinkedIn and other job boards

LinkedIn will allow you to search for jobs and set these searches up as job alerts. You can select the frequency of notification. I suggest setting up a job alert by using as many titles as possible that could be suitable and interesting to you.

Share your career interests with recruiters

You can let recruiters know that you are open to new opportunities. This will be visible to corporate as well as agency recruiters. It will **not be visible** to anyone in your organisation.

Discover the 'hidden' job market

The hidden job market refers to jobs that exist right now and will appear as vacancies soon, but are not publicly advertised. They are known only to a small group of stakeholders in the organisation.

In my experience, at least around a third of jobs at mid- to high-income levels are filled without the roles being publicly announced on any job boards. This is why it's essential to find out about these jobs before they go public and get competitive. Get ahead of the line and get engaged in a meaningful discovery conversation early on in the process.

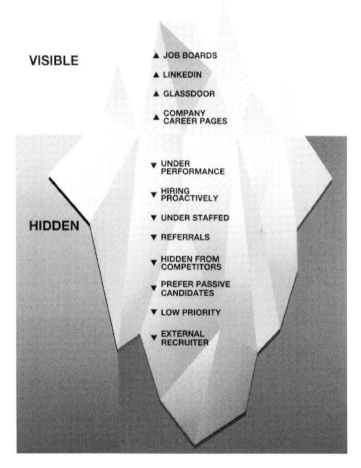

VISIBLE

▲ JOB BOARDS

▲ LINKEDIN

▲ GLASSDOOR

▲ COMPANY CAREER PAGES

▼ UNDER PERFORMANCE

▼ HIRING PROACTIVELY

▼ UNDER STAFFED

HIDDEN

▼ REFERRALS

▼ HIDDEN FROM COMPETITORS

▼ PREFER PASSIVE CANDIDATES

▼ LOW PRIORITY

▼ EXTERNAL RECRUITER

The hidden job market

There are two stages involved in the hidden job market process.

1. Before a formal job vacancy is established

These positions don't exist yet, but it's highly probable they will within the next sixty to ninety days. Here are a few reasons why:

- **Under-performance.** The incumbent is still in the position, but they are under-performing (and this is not expected to change).

- **Extended leave.** The incumbent is currently on medical or maternity leave and there is a reasonable probability that they may not return from leave, so the manager wants to be prepared and may be open to a contractual arrangement.

- **Hiring proactively.** The company is in growth mode, well-funded and willing to hire proactively when it has identified the right person.

- **Under-staffed.** The team is overworked and under-staffed, so there is a need for the position. Even though it's not formally approved, the company will expedite approval if it identifies the right person.

2. After a formal job vacancy is established

These positions are approved and open for hire right now, but they are not advertised on job boards. Here are a few reasons why:

- **Referral preference.** The company has a strong preference for internal referrals because they are recommendations versus unknown job advertising applicants.

- **Passive preference.** The hiring manager prefers passive candidates who don't have a strong push factor from their current role versus candidates actively seeking a new job.

- **Lower priority.** The HR/talent acquisition team is under resourced and has too many jobs to fill, so a few jobs are either lower priority, lower urgency or the hiring manager has a few people in mind already.

- **External recruitment.** The hiring manager is using a head hunter who doesn't use job ads for the position because the skills required are rare or they have a strong pool of candidates they can contact quickly.

- **Competitive intelligence.** The company doesn't want its competitors to know it is hiring for the position.

The top four benefits of knowing about the hidden job market are:

1. **Fewer candidates.** You are engaging in a one-to-one or a one-to-few hiring process because there's likely to be a small pool of candidates known to the stakeholders, including internal candidates.

2. **More engagement.** The fewer the candidates, the more attention, engagement and time you will get from the hiring manager and stakeholders.

3. **Better assessment of fit.** The more time you get with the hiring manager and stakeholders, the more likely you are to get additional information about the organisation's culture, strategy and financial performance as well as the people you would be working with on a daily basis. This helps you make a fully informed decision about the fit and MVP.

4. **Greater chances of reaching agreement.** Fewer candidates, more engagement and better assessment of fit enable both parties to value each other. The more value the organisation and hiring manager see in you, and you in them, the better likelihood you have of being able to negotiate the terms of work, such as salary, benefits, flexibility and balance, that are important to you.

Let's finish this chapter with eight best practices for job-search success:

1. Research companies, contacts and jobs

2. Write and update your target contact list frequently

3. At a minimum, adopt a weekly search activity planning cycle

4. Set up job alerts, check every day and apply for roles

5. Use LinkedIn to see if you are connected to anyone at the company that is advertising, then reach out to them and ask for an internal referral

6. Block out time for an appointment with yourself to work on your job search as a priority activity

7. Use a journal to manage your search project and capture your reflections, ideas, information and actions

8. If you lack motivation, find an accountability partner, mentor or coach who is more driven than you, has successfully been through this process and can dramatically improve your mindset, actions and results

SWITCH ACTION

Having completed this chapter, write down at least one thing you've learned and one action you need to take. You may like to use the Switch actions sheet at www.switch.work/bonus to record your learning points and action plan.

ELEVEN

Get Out Of The Job Queue And Connect With People

PRINCIPLE

Switch from the shadows into the spotlight.

Do you like queues? I don't – I hate them! So why wait in an online queue to find your next job, only be added to a long list of people to be reviewed (and reviewed some more), contacted, screened etc? I'm sure you get my point.

I've now been an executive recruiter for over a decade, working with major corporate hiring managers, and I know that there are much more effective ways to get a new role than just responding to job ads. How many times have you looked at a job ad and thought about whether you should apply or not? Then you decide to apply, but you need to tweak and update your resume and write your covering letter, so you think some more and wait some more, applying a few days later. But guess what? There are 357 other people ahead of you, all applying for the same job.

Good luck!

What if there was a way of going right up to the front of the queue, having the right conversation and asking the right questions to get what you want? I'm here to let you know that there is. Whether you are excited or feel challenged by this possibility, you can save yourself a lot of time, so choose to swim against the tide and stand out from the pack.

Stand out from the pack

People know people and that has a compounding effect for your network and its reach within the industry, whether you remain in your current role and industry or change to something new. If you're like most people, you will feel some degree of resistance to asking others for help. This can range from minor resistance (where you do it anyway) to major resistance, where you procrastinate and don't do it.

Let me ask you to consider this question – would you invest $1 on the odds that you could get a $2 return? Or maybe, to up the value, would you invest $1,000 on the odds that you could get a $5,000 return? I know I'd say yes.

Now if I said, 'Would you invest in an action that has a discomfort level of two, three, four or five out of ten to get a return of seven, eight, nine or ten out of ten?' **Surely you would if there was a low risk investment to get a high-return and high-reward outcome.** So, just do it – ask people. At worst they will say no or not respond. At best, you could get the job you want.

SWITCH TIP

Courage is the ability to take action despite fear and resistance.

How to connect with people

Yes, we need to talk about this. The way we communicate for work has dramatically changed over the last decade. People are far more informal than before, which is good news for you because you may not have to deal with the challenging 'gate-keepers' any longer. People are more visible and accessible as well. There is almost always a way (if there is a will) to contact the person you want to connect with.

Channels of communication:

- **In person**. This is the richest form of communication that uses all senses.

- **Video/conference calls**. These offer in-person connection over distance and include Zoom, Skype, Google Hangouts and FaceTime.

- **Phone**. This is popular and influential, but it is challenging trying to reach people during prime office hours.

- **Email**. This is still popular and allows both parties to think before communicating, but there are lower opening rates and restrictions as a result of spam filters.

- **Text messages**. These are mainstream at work and highly effective because they are instant with near 100% open rates. Texts can be exchanged at any time and allow both parties to think before communicating.

- **Social chat apps** (eg WhatsApp). These are growing in popularity.

- **Internet message**. These are boards for groups and provide the ability for members to message one-on-one.

- **Social networks**. LinkedIn messaging is currently the most predominant for work.

SWITCH TIP

LinkedIn is an invaluable tool when it comes to connecting, staying in touch and contacting people you know, and those with whom you want to connect and network.

The AIM model – securing interviews

AIM stands for aware, interested and motivated. I use this three-step model to make hiring managers and stakeholders aware of candidates who could be of benefit to them and be relevant for a position they are hiring for at that time, or will be in the near future. I also recommend this as a tool for you to use in your job-search journey. If there's an opportunity people are aware of, they will either redirect you, introduce you or tell the relevant people about you. Then you are much more likely to secure the right interview/s.

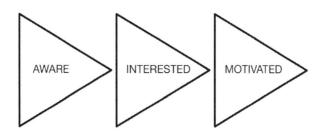

The AIM model

Here's how the three-step AIM model works.

Step 1: Aware. Contact people to make them aware that you are exploring new job opportunities. The first and biggest hurdle to overcome here is awareness. You are not aware of all the suitable jobs that exist at the moment. Vice versa, the people hiring for jobs who require your experience don't know that you are currently interested in their job.

Everyone is busy and focused on achieving goals and overcoming challenges, and even the people who know you and care about you might not be aware that you are dissatisfied in your current job or that you are in between jobs. This is the reason why you need to contact them and connect with them. At this first step in the model, you need to be proactive, targeted and persistent in contacting the right people.

Step 2: Interested. Educate people about why you're interested in working with them, the company or the role, and how you're a good match for them. Highlight relevant problems you've solved and results you've achieved through a STAR story. In addition, mention people you have in common – this is a great ice-breaker.

Be careful to ensure that you know the person in common well enough and that they have a positive relationship with the hiring manager. You can quickly figure this out with a call, text or email to the person in common. If there's an opportunity that they know of in their team, company or industry for which you are a good fit, most people will be interested in communicating with you, as well as others they know would benefit.

Step 3: Motivated. You can motivate people by including a call to action. Be specific about what you want them to do next.

Scarcity and timing are two factors that motivate people to take action. In terms of scarcity, if you have a rare skill, it is useful to point out that there are more jobs than candidates for a skill like that. In the case of timing, if you are available to start straight away, this could spur people into action. In addition, depending on the maturity and stage of your other job opportunities, you could mention that you may not be available too much longer. This demonstrates that you are motivated to explore opportunities in a timely manner.

People who are AIMed

When people are aware, interested and motivated, they will respond positively by informing you of one or a number of opportunities that you can act on. For example:

- They are hiring for the position that interests you

- They know someone in their company who is hiring for the position that interests you

- They know someone outside their company who is hiring for the position that interests you

- They know of a company that is hiring because they were approached, but are not sure whom to contact at the company

- They know a recruiter who is well networked in your target industry or company and specialises in the position that interests you

SWITCH TIP

Getting people aware, interested and motivated is the fastest way to secure an interview.

Work your network

Here is a list of people you can approach and potentially connect with, from the warmest to the coolest contacts in terms of relational capital.

People you know:

- Friends

- Past colleagues

- Partners and collaborators

- Customers

- School and university friends

- Industry group acquaintances

- Known industry recruiters.

People at companies that are on your target list:

- Hiring managers

- Stakeholders, including HR and talent acquisition teams

- LinkedIn connections in common with the hiring manager and stakeholders

- Advocates and influencers

- Contacts you've met at conferences and events

- Corporate recruiters

But what if:

- **People don't reply?** They probably aren't aware of an opportunity and are too busy to reply now, or may intend to do it later, but don't. Either way, they are aware you are looking. If anyone contacts them, they can refer you. You're ahead.

- **People aren't interested?** They don't think you are a good fit or there isn't a need for your experience at this time. That can change in a moment when a different role comes up for which you could be a great fit, and then the interest level goes up. You're still winning.

- **People reply and suggest next steps?** You have accomplished your goal at this stage. You have secured an interview. You've won.

Find out more about how to navigate hiring managers, HR and recruiters and additional tips on securing the interview at www.switch.work/bonus.

SWITCH ACTION

Having completed this chapter, write down at least one thing you've learned and one action you need to take. You may like to use the Switch actions sheet at www.switch.work/bonus to record your learning points and action plan.

SECTION FIVE
INTERVIEW
INFLUENCE

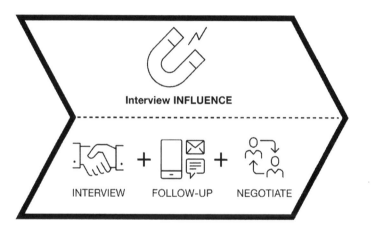

Interview **INFLUENCE**

INTERVIEW + FOLLOW-UP + NEGOTIATE

TWELVE

Consultative Interviews Create Influence

PRINCIPLE

Switch from simply answering questions to influencing the outcome.

Think about the last time you went to see a doctor. Did they prescribe the medicine before or after understanding what the problem was with you? They likely asked you a series of questions, considered the symptoms, diagnosed the problem, and only then recommended how they would treat or solve the problem.

That's a consultation. A doctor will find out what the problem is before advising solutions so they get it right, because there is no room for error when it comes to your health. In the same way, a consultative interview requires you to be the doctor and discover the needs of the hiring manager before providing a solution to their problem.

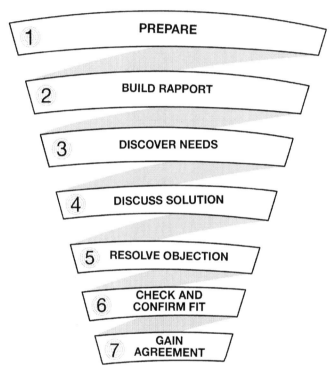

The seven-step consultative interview process

These needs could be problems to be solved or goals that the hiring manager wants to achieve in the role you are interviewing for. By discovering exactly what they are, you are likely to provide the right information to the hiring manager without missing the mark, which enables you both to assess whether you are a good fit for the role or not. It also gives you the best opportunity to exert influence because you know exactly what the role needs to achieve and can demonstrate how you would succeed in it.

There are seven steps in a consultative interview:

1. Prepare

2. Build rapport

3. Discover needs

4. Discuss solutions

5. Resolve objections

6. Check and confirm fit

7. Gain agreement

SWITCH TIP

Prescription without diagnosis is malpractice.

Step 1. Prepare

Yes, we need to talk about this, especially if you're the type to say, 'I was born ready.' And my reply? 'No, you weren't.' Let me show you how to prepare for the interview.

Preparation is the first and most essential step in the seven-step interview process. It not only prevents poor performance, it also enables you to have the perfect start to an interview where you build rapport with the hiring manager to set up the environment for exchanging meaningful information.

The more desirable the job, the **greater the expectation and competition**. The biggest benefit of preparation is being ready to consult and influence during the interview, based on the knowledge you have brought from external and internal resources into your current awareness. External resources come from people, research on LinkedIn and Google, job description details etc. Internal resources come from your memory, experience and intuition. This information is stored in your short-term conscious memory and is ready to share at the interview.

10/10 interview preparation checklist

Here is a list of ten areas of things you need to know, including some sources of information I recommend in relation to preparing for your interview:

1. **Company.** To learn more about the company, use Google as a starting point.

2. **People**. To learn more about the person/people you will be meeting in the interview, use LinkedIn as a starting point.

3. **Job role**. To learn more about the role, use the job description. If possible, speak with the recruiter

or referrer, or any other informer or advocate within the company.

4. **Dress code**. Enquire and/or decide whether to dress up or dress down for the interview.

5. **Directions**. Ensure you have the address of where your interview is being held, and have researched and decided how and when you will arrive. Getting to your meeting five to ten minutes in advance is critical.

6. **Rapport builders**. Research what you have in common that could build rapport with the person/people you are meeting (eg acquaintances, companies, locations, activities, interests).

7. **Your questions**. Have a list of questions prepared for the person/people you are meeting that only they can answer for you.

8. **Their questions**. Be prepared to answer the most common questions people ask when holding interviews.

9. **STAR stories**. These will help you stand out from the crowd. Detail real-life work challenges and the results/outcomes you delivered in the context of these stories. Ensure you prepare three stories that are relevant to the job role, including the situation, tension, action and results (STAR).

10. **MVP fit**. This is the combination of what you want (and the potential employer will offer you in the EVP) and what they want (and you

offer through your PVP). Come to the interview prepared having thought about this fit, which makes for a powerful MVP for both you and the potential employer.

You can find a template for the 10/10 preparation checklist at www.switch.work/bonus.

Step 2. Build rapport

Why build rapport with the interviewer?

Rapport is responsiveness, which is a highly desirable state in any relationship. Maximum responsiveness enables the best exchange of information and ideas. This is essential for you and the person or people you meet at interview to determine whether each of you is the right fit for the other.

Rapport is the connection and spark that we all desire in interactions. People like people they are like and want to be like – people with whom they have commonality and familiarity. And they hire people they are like. This is a key factor to remember when you're building rapport.

SWITCH TIP

Rapport is the highway to influence.

But this can be restrictive because there are a lot of people out there who *aren't* exactly like you or like the same things. To overcome this restriction, you need to have the skill and behavioural variety to build rapport with anyone, and quickly when you're in thirty- to sixty-minute interviews.

People judge people in a matter of seconds. Fortunately (or unfortunately), first impressions matter. You might say that you can't always be your authentic self in an interview situation and you would be right, but the reality is rapport will likely influence the outcome of the interview. Depending on how much you want the specific job, you will have to decide how hard you are prepared to work to build rapport with the person or people you meet.

SWITCH TIP

The person with the most behavioural flexibility exerts the most influence on the outcome.

According to Albert Mehrabian, Professor Emeritus of Psychology at the University of California, Los Angeles, communication is made up of:[1]

- 7% words

- 38% tone of voice

- 55% body language

---

1 Wikipedia contributors, 'Albert Mehrabian', *Wikipedia, The Free Encyclopedia*, 4 September 2019, https://en.wikipedia.org/wiki/Albert_Mehrabian [accessed 16 January 2020]

These three elements account for our liking or disliking of the person in front of us. The most important factor to keep in mind is that they should be congruent and support each other. It would be weird to have a big friendly smile on your face, but have your arms tightly folded across your chest as a barrier.

Matching and mirroring

The technique of matching and mirroring was pioneered in the fifties and sixties by Dr Milton Erickson, a renowned psychologist and hypnotherapist He spent years studying the unconscious mind and was famous for creating instant rapport and achieving dramatic breakthroughs with people.

To help create rapport with the interviewer, match and mirror them in subtle ways. You need to be acutely aware of their behaviour, and then find common ground that builds on this rapport. The components of communication include the words you speak, your tone of voice and your body language.

Words:

- A great place to start is to talk about the weather and people you know who you have in common.

- Based on the environment and situational opportunity, find a common launch point to converse about places, activities, interests, industry events, news, entertainment, sports, kids, holidays etc. Pick one of these topics and discuss it for two to three minutes.

- If the interviewer talks about vision and strategy, use the same words when responding – the exact words and phrases they use.

Tone of voice:

- If they speak loudly, speak up

- If they are softly spoken, speak more softly than normal

- If they are fast talkers, speed up your pace of talking

- If they are slow talkers, take it easy and slow down your pace of talking

Body language:

- If they lean forward, gradually lean forward too

- If they are animated with their hands, liven up yourself

- If they are comfortable, reclining with legs crossed, gradually get comfortable and cross your legs

These are suggestions to help you get maximum responsiveness and cooperation from the people you meet at interview, but please don't implement all of them at once. They're meant to make the other person feel comfortable and to help you find common ground with them, but if you are overtly uncrossing your arms or scratching your ear when they do, the interview could get awkward very quickly. Be mindful that 93% of communication consists of body language (55%) and tone of voice (38%), so these two components are critical in the process of building credibility and rapport.

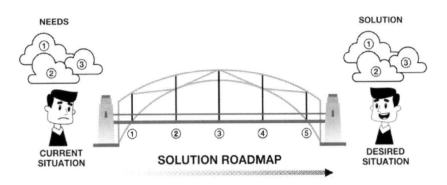

Consultative framework

The Consultative Interview Framework

This framework is at the heart of consultative interviews. At its core, it is about...

- Discovering the needs of the people interviewing you, which are made up of:

  » The current situation and their existing needs, motives and problems (step 3)

  » The desired situation in the future and solutions for their problems as well as the goals they want to achieve (step 4)

» Identifying and analysing the gap between current and desired solutions

• Discussing how you can help them with solutions to their problems and achieve their goals

... to suggest a roadmap for moving forward (gap identification) and to help them achieve their goals and objectives (their desired situation).

SWITCH TIP

Help others get what they want and you will have what you want.

Step 3. Discover needs

Having established rapport with the interviewer, you can start to ask questions to discover their needs in the role for which you are being interviewed. You could bridge the conversation from a light topic to discovering their needs by saying something like:

'I appreciate you meeting me today. I've been looking forward to learning more about the goals you want to achieve and the challenges you want to overcome through this role. Would you like to ask me some questions first or may I ask you some questions?'

This tells them that you are focused on their agenda and would like to find out more about it (before talking about yourself), which is the ideal situation. You want to know exactly what the challenges and goals are so that you can specifically address how you can help to achieve them. Everything else outside of this is irrelevant to the interviewer(s) and will be forgotten.

They are likely to tell you more about the role, challenges and goals instead of asking you questions about yourself (before you know exactly what their pain points are). This positions you as a consultative and caring professional, so please find out their needs before you talk about yourself or how you can help them achieve their goals.

You will find that most needs are centred around the five hiring motives, and you can safely assume that every single position in an organisation – small or large – will be operating and fuelled by these motives for itself or others:

- **Gain or profit**. The position exists to grow revenue and profits (eg sales).

- **Fear of loss**. The position exists to save money (eg finance).

- **Satisfaction and comfort**. The position exists to make things better or easier (eg HR, customer services).

- **Peace of mind**. The position exists to make things more secure (eg IT security).

- **Pride and prestige**. The position exists to make the company look good in the world (eg marketing).

When you have permission to go ahead and ask questions to find out more about the interviewer's needs for the position, I recommend you ask:

Discovery questions

Current situation questions

Ask, probe and listen to what the current factors are in the role. If you don't understand something, clarify it and go deeper. Sometimes it takes four to five questions to get to the heart of a matter. You can also ask about how satisfied the interviewers are right now about the way things are.

Here are some sample questions to ask to help you understand the current realities:

- What are the top three challenges or problems you would like the person to tackle in this role?

- How is this impacting the team and the customer?

- Who are the key stakeholders in the role?

- How long has this been a problem?

- Why did this position become available?

Desired situation questions

Ask, probe and listen to what goals and outcomes the interviewer desires in the role. Sometimes you can achieve the highest mileage by identifying what the interviewer really wants to achieve and their 'What's in it for me?' factor. What are the implications for the interviewer personally? You can then show how you could help them achieve their ideal outcome.

Here are some sample questions to ask to help you understand and achieve the desired goals:

- What are the top three outcomes and goals you would like to achieve?

- What are the timeframes in which these need to be achieved?

- What has been done so far towards achieving these outcomes and goals?

- What is the impact of success on the team and customer/s?

- What changes do you anticipate in the next three to six months in this role?

Analyse the gap

Once you can see the gap between where the interviewers are and where they want to be, you are in a position to show them how you will take them from their current situation to their desired situation. You can then bridge the gap by discussing the solution.

This is how you demonstrate value and exert influence in an interview process.

SWITCH TIP

At the core of every mid-level to senior job, people are looking for solutions to problems and results to be achieved.

Step 4. Discuss Solutions

The higher you go in an organisation, the broader the responsibility, the wider the impact and the greater the stakes. This simply means that if you are upwardly mobile, you are likely to interview with senior executives for your next role. They are typically under pressure, overworked and goal-oriented. They want problems solved and goals achieved, and the interview is a means to find the right person to do this. So once you discover their needs and have identified the gap/s, you can then tell them about how you are going to solve their problems and help them achieve their goals using the five steps of the solution proposal roadmap.

Solution roadmap to bridge the gap

You can make a big impact on your interviewers when you tell them exactly how you would solve their problem if you were to get the job. Here is a five-step roadmap to follow to discuss solutions and bridge the gap from current situation to desired situation.

1. Structure. If you structure what you have to say, it simplifies your message and increases recall.

2. Describe. Explain how you would solve each problem and bridge the gap by providing three to five steps, describing the sequence of actions you would take. Share specific measurements and timeframes you would expect, mention who you would involve and what you would need from the company.

3. Build credibility. Anyone can talk about what they will do in the future. What gives those plans weight are the results you have already accomplished and other reputable sources who will endorse you. You can build credibility into your solution propositions by including:

- Your STAR stories from current and past roles where you solved a similar problem or achieved a similar goal

- Proof that demonstrates past success

- Name dropping by offering well-known customer success references

- Name dropping by offering former managerial references and endorsements

- Formal recognition you have received in third-party media

- Awards you have received

Use people, companies, dates, product names, sales figures, ratings, comments and other quantitative measurements. These make you credible and your story memorable. Continuously collect support material for your future interviews – reports, statistics, news items, reference letters and testimonials. These create high impact during the meeting as well as the follow-up stage.

4. Summarise. When you summarise your solution, it reinforces and solidifies it in the interviewers' understanding.

5. Feedback. Seeking feedback helps you to plan the next step/s based on one of three scenarios:

- Scenario 1: if the interviewers are in complete agreement, suggest next steps

- Scenario 2: if they need more information, it gives you the opportunity to provide it to them

- Scenario 3: if they are not in agreement or have an objection, it gives you the opportunity to resolve it

Solution roadmap example:

> 'About three years ago, I walked into a similar situation where the top sales person had resigned because she wasn't successful in getting the manager's role and the team had been disengaged for a while. This was causing the company to lose $1 million a month and management was considering reducing the workforce by 20%.

It was stressful and negative.

'I started by building an authentic and supportive relationship with my team, acknowledging the problems and asking them to come on the journey with me to solve them. I didn't have all the answers, but together, we did. I also gained commitment from each team member to achieve a weekly total of ten meetings booked and completed with new customers (formerly this was three to five meetings per team member). I introduced the ability to finish the day early on Fridays, if they achieved their targets.

'We saw a doubling in activity and the resulting pipeline in forty-five days. Within ninety days, we achieved our monthly sales targets for the first time in twelve months. Within a year, we registered our first 100% of targets and 30% year-over-year growth. This set us up for a record year the following year. You can call John Watts, the senior vice president, who moved to another company last year. He will confirm this outcome (build credibility).

'In summary, I know that I can achieve the region's targets in three phases. Firstly, with increasing team engagement, then doubling the team's activity, and finally pipeline management. How does that sound to you (seek feedback)?'

SWITCH TIP

The most important question in the hiring manager's mind is 'What can you do for me?' Do not leave the interview without answering this.

Step 5. Resolve objections

Objections arise when there is a gap between the interviewer's expectations and understanding of reality. Sometimes there is a genuine gap, and at other times it is a lack of understanding on their part or communication on your part. Either way, you will face objections verbally or in body language during the interview process (eg defensive posture, disinterest etc).

The two types of objection you will encounter are:

1. Objections due to factual gaps

2. Objections due to perceived gaps

Learning how to resolve these objections (think 're-solve') means having another attempt or approach at solving a problem, and this helps you to:

• Manage prickly situations

• Answer difficult questions

• Handle confrontational situations

- Navigate oppositional negotiations more effectively

- Suggest positive solutions to problems

- Progress to gaining agreement

Objection resolution framework

1. Acknowledge. This shows that you have heard the objection and are eager to resolve it. It diffuses resistance and the potential for conflict, setting the right atmosphere for further discussion rather than reaching an uncomfortable impasse.

2. Discover concerns and hidden needs. Ask, listen and probe. Asking questions helps you understand the concerns and the needs behind the concerns. Then resolve the concerns by addressing the unmet need. The more you discover and meet needs, the more confidence you will build with the interviewer. They will want to work with you because they'll have had a one-on-one consultative problem-solving conversation with a professional.

3. Resolution discussion. Provide a structured, descriptive solution or explanation. Refer to credible external sources who will further confirm to the interviewer that you meet their need and they shouldn't be concerned. The goal is to turn the concern into comfort and, if possible, into confidence.

$$\text{Concern} \longrightarrow \text{Comfort} \longrightarrow \text{Confidence}$$

If the same objection comes up with another stake-holder, you can then repeat your answer and refer to the previous interviewer as being 'comfortable' or 'confident' with your response.

4. Seek feedback about the solution you have just provided. Did it meet the interviewer's needs and satisfy their concerns? Have they moved from concern to comfort?

SWITCH TIP

You will be infinitely more successful in your career when you master resolving objections. Most people get stuck and can't navigate an objection.

Top five objections that come up during the interview process

1. You feel that the concerns are to do with your age, but the interviewer will not acknowledge it in the interview. You will need to read between the lines and observe the demographics within the office. Decide if you want the job, and if you do, talk about how you relate well with younger people and the benefits of your experience to the team. Say that people don't feel competitive with you, and that allows you to be a positive mentor and help others succeed as well.

2. The salary is much lower than you expected and need. Don't compromise – keep pursuing other roles. If you do accept the offer, make a commitment with the hiring manager for a period of time that you will remain in the role, and stay true to it.

3. The hiring manager has had a bad experience with another employee from your current company. Ask them if everyone in their company is 100% identical in thought, behaviour and results – surely not. Gently remind them that it is an unfair comparison.

4. The hiring manager says you are not the right cultural fit. Take this as a blessing. You probably don't want to try to convince someone who knows the team well enough and the dynamics that obviously exist. Why pursue it further?

5. The hiring manager won't bring up objections during the interview. They may want to avoid confrontation as details of this may be communicated back through HR or to a recruiter. If you have developed rapport and mutual responsiveness throughout the interview, you have earned the right to ask what concerns they have. Or you could ask them what obstacles and issues would prevent you from being successful in the job or as part of the team. This is a good way to confirm that there isn't anything that could hinder your progress.

Step 6. Check and confirm fit

Now that you have prepared, built rapport, discovered needs, discussed solutions and resolved objections (if they've come up), it's time to check whether the interviewer is comfortable, or better still, confident about the fit.

Most people are used to walking out of an interview uncertain about whether or not they are a good fit for the role, especially when they are told, 'We'll get back to you.' But why wait and wonder? Ask the interviewer/s what they think. Checking is a powerful consultative skill and a simple but mighty tool in that:

- You'll know if the interviewers think you are a good fit

- You'll know if they think you aren't a good fit

- You'll have an opportunity to resolve any misconceptions

- You'll have the best chance of influencing them in person and reaching agreement

So go ahead and ask, 'Based on our conversation today, how do you feel or what do you think about my fit for the role?' At this stage, they can say:

- Scenario 1: 'I think you are a good fit'

- Scenario 2: 'I think you could be a good fit, but…' (an objection)

- Scenario 3: 'I think you aren't a good fit because…' (an objection)

- Scenario 4: 'I/HR/the recruiter will get back to you' (delayed feedback)

In response to scenarios 2 and 3 where an objection is raised, revert to the objection resolution framework and go through the four steps of:

- Acknowledge

- Discover needs and problems

- Resolve

- Seek feedback

In response to scenarios 1 and 4, which are positive or neutral, and/or once you have resolved the outstanding objection, it is your turn to confirm the fit (your MVP). The key focus of this final part of the interview is to confirm, in both your mind and the mind of the interviewer, your understanding of:

- EVP – what they offer you. Help them to understand your PVP.

- PVP – what you offer them. What is the MVP?

- MVP – how could this be a successful mutually beneficial partnership?

You can find more information about this in Chapter 6.

Checking and confirming fit framework

1. Mention research before and during the meeting. This demonstrates that your assessment of fit is well considered.

2. Communicate how your values, experience, education and past results will be essential in helping the interviewer or the company bridge the gap, solving their problems and achieving goals. You can keep this high level (generic) or detailed and specific.

3. Explain what it is about the job that interests you. Don't leave them wondering if you are interested, tell them. People are likely to match confidence and interest (as well as the lack of it).

4. Mention that you would be better together. Each of you is an equal partner, bringing something that the other values and needs. This is the best level playing-field statement.

Here is a sample framework script you could use to wrap up the interview:

'Thank you for an informative and enjoyable interview today. Based on my prior research and what I have learned during our interview, I am confident that I will bring the values, experience and past success to repair and build customer relationships, improve team morale and achieve regional goals. You offer the culture, leadership, recognition and growth opportunities that interest me. This is the right fit for us both and together we can collaborate to do great things/grow this company/dominate the market/make a big difference etc.'

SWITCH TIP

Maintain an even keel posture where you are confident, interested, aware of the value you bring, clear of the value the interviewers bring and how these could work really well together. People like people who have clarity and direction.

Step 7. Gain agreement

Gaining agreement at the end of each interview ensures that you will be able to progress in the interview process to the final stage, as well as eventually securing the job. This process of agreement involves two steps:

1. **Asking to take the next step**. Enthusiastically and confidently ask the interviewer what the next step will look like and whether you can proceed to it.

2. **Being comfortable with silence**. This allows the interviewer to think clearly about the question you have asked and prompts a response.

The process of securing a job (the big agreement) is made up of numerous sequential small agreements such as gaining a referral, agreeing to a phone call, securing another interview, shaking hands to move forward to the next stage and moving people from being uncertain about your fit to being confident about it.

SWITCH TIP

Never finish a meeting without gaining a small or big agreement.

Find the top 10 most common interview questions with responses at www.switch.work/bonus.

SWITCH ACTION

Having completed this chapter, write down at least one thing you've learned and one action you need to take. You may like to use the Switch actions sheet at www.switch.work/bonus to record your learning points and action plan.

THIRTEEN

Follow Up To Stay Top Of Mind

PRINCIPLE

Switch from silence to momentum.

Once you've been to your interview, it's time to review how it went. I recommend four essential steps:

1. Reflect on the interview

2. Follow up on next steps

3. Complete further research

4. Keep exploring new roles

Reflect on the interview

Once you have left the interview site, it's time to decide when you are going to review the meeting. Some people will call their spouses, a loved one or a friend, and others call the external recruiter who set up the interview, but neither of these is a substitute for the reflection and assessment you need to do afterwards. This is a critical step for maintaining your clarity, even though you may have been in a high degree of rapport and responsiveness with the hiring manager.

Most of us have many commitments and responsibilities to navigate on a daily basis, and if it isn't another meeting we need to attend, we're on our computers and mobile devices, responding to texts, emails and calls. Then the day and its demands overtake our attention and we go home and just want to unwind – over and out. Next day we launch into a similar routine, and as one day turns into another, we forget vital pieces of information that will help us in determining whether or not the job we're considering is the right fit.

Taking the time to reflect as soon as possible after your interview is vital in assessing and deciding what your next steps will be. It will also help you stand out as a top candidate, otherwise you will just be another me-too candidate among numerous options. The best times to reflect and journal about a job interview are:

- Immediately after the meeting

- In your car or at a café on the same day

- Before you arrive home at the end of that day (unless you live alone)

- Before you go to bed that night

- The next morning before getting into the day (if the day before options didn't work)

You can use some of the suggestions coming up to assist you in this reflection process, including which questions to reflect upon, journaling and the traffic light assessment.

Interview reflection questions

- What were your goals for this interview?

- To what extent did you achieve them?

- What did you do well in this interview?

- What new information did you learn at this interview?

- What new questions and concerns have come up during this interview?

- How does this job meet what you are looking for in a new role?

- How do this company's values align with yours? Where are the gaps?

- To what extent would this company and industry offer you opportunity for growth?

- What would you have liked to say, but didn't get a chance to due to time restrictions?

- What would you have liked to ask, but didn't get a chance to due to time restrictions?

- Given another chance, what would you do differently in this interview?

On a scale of 1–10 (10 being the highest), how would you rate:

- The company values and their fit to your values?

- The role and its fit to your interests and experience/strengths?

- The hiring manager and the fit between their management style and your working preferences?

- The compensation and benefits package on offer and its fit to your current structure?

- The benefits that you desire but can't quantify (eg proximity to home, flexibility, travel, learning opportunities etc)?

Based on all the information above, how does this role fit you?

SWITCH TIP

Take a minimum of fifteen minutes to work through as many of the interview reflection questions as you can. The best way to do this is by writing your responses in a question and answer format. Use a journal to write down your thoughts and assess them against your values and goal.

You can find an interview reflection template at www.switch.work/bonus.

Why journal?

I talked about journaling and the benefits of alone time in Chapter Four, and I recommend you refer back to this. There's a strong connection between writing things down and evoking mindfulness. Journaling brings the interview into the present moment, moving past the distractions of the day and the demands that will be there tomorrow. This will help you notice things that you learned but didn't necessarily pay enough attention to.

Journaling can also be useful to achieve an advantage in a role you want, as well as to avoid a job that may have initially sounded great, but actually doesn't align with your values and is therefore a bad fit. It will give you confidence whether you progress with the interview or not, or whether the company decides to move forward without you. Either way, you will have some really valuable thoughts and notes you can refer back to.

Traffic light assessment

This assessment tool is another means by which you can reflect upon your interview experience to determine if the company, team and job role are right for you.

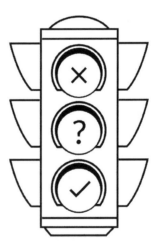

Reflecting on your interview and the job role, write down your responses in the space provided under the three traffic light prompts. The table can be downloaded from www.switch.work/bonus.

Traffic light table

Green light	Yellow light	Red light
What do you like, and what aligns well with you?	What are you unsure about in terms of alignment with you?	What don't you like, and what doesn't align with you?

Once you've written down responses to the traffic light prompts in the table, review each of the areas further by taking these actions:

Green light: check that you have all the correct information you need. Can you validate this with someone who was not part of the interview process?

Yellow light: research this area further. Ask for more information from influencers and informers (people you know and with whom you have a good relationship within the organisation), including an informal meeting with a peer or stakeholder. Also talk to your advisors.

Red light: divide your responses into major and minor concerns. Do your concerns affect your peace of mind, security, convenience and ability to achieve goals on a daily basis? If yes, then withdraw graciously. If no, research and get more information about minor concerns.

Follow up on next steps

Go/no-go decision

Based on your responses to the traffic light prompts and review of this information, together with your reflections and journaling, decide whether the role is a:

- **Go:** proceed with the next steps forward to follow up this role

- **No-go:** do not proceed any further with pursuing this role

Do this for each interview you attend, as well as for subsequent interviews for the same role.

If you decide the role is a no-go:

- Send an email to the person who is managing the recruitment process informing them you don't wish to proceed

- Keep it simple/to the point so it's not taken personally or defensively by the receiver

- An example of this brief email could be, 'After reflection and further consideration, I don't think this role is the right fit for me'

If you decide the role is a go:

- Send a follow-up email the next day, or at the latest the day after (once you have had your reflection/journaling time) using the follow-up communication framework.

- I don't recommend an email the same day because it appears too eager, and may communicate that you are desperate and haven't taken time to reflect on whether or not this role is right for you.

- On the other hand, sending an email five to seven days later seems like a bit of an after-thought.

- I recommend not sending handwritten notes, because again they may show that you are too eager, and possibly desperate. They also take too long to get to the recipient.

- If you made suggestions in the interview about how you can solve the company's problems and achieve its goals, it's a great idea to follow this up in your email.

- I don't recommend the basic 'thank-you' email because you then position yourself as less important – equals don't communicate like this. Remain an equal.

Follow-up communication framework

You can use this framework to craft a great email that will remind the hiring manager of and reinforce the value and fit you offer to the company.

1. Recap fit

2. Remind them what interests you

3. Attach relevant information

4. Refer to common connections

5. Ask further questions (limit these)

Follow up with a note or a call to the recruitment process owner and your point of contact – HR, internal recruiter, hiring manager or the external recruiter – as this demonstrates interest and responsiveness (rapport), which is likely to be matched by them.

Here is a sample email that uses the follow-up communication framework:

'Hi Belinda,

I enjoyed meeting you yesterday and the conversation we had. Your current challenges are well aligned to my experience and I am excited about the opportunity to make a difference by building the right team, turning around key customer relationships and achieving regional goals after a two-year drought.

I've attached a one-page summary with three to five bullet points on how I would achieve your three main objectives in a thirty-, sixty- and ninety-day timeframe. In addition to this, I've attached a success story about how I took my previous team to record-breaking results for the first time, achieving 100% of targets and 30% year-over-year growth.

You can speak to John Watts, the senior vice president of the company at the time, on <insert contact number>. Here is his profile <insert LinkedIn profile>.

There is just one question that I meant to ask: can you tell me what the current level of marketing/lead generation support is in the region? I would welcome a conversation with you or the marketing lead when it is appropriate.

Best regards,

<insert your name>'

Complete further research

Following your interview, it is essential you continue researching the company, its people and the role so you can find out as much as possible. Take these steps as part of your further research:

- Search for more information regarding areas of interest, as well as any areas of concern you may have.

- Talk to people you know within the company (informers and influencers) who can give you more information.

- Talk to your advisors and tell them what it is you know and have found out about the company and job role. Ask them what they think about the fit.

- Connect on LinkedIn. This will help you to:

  » See/find people you have in common

  » The interviewers will see any assets you have on your profile (that they hadn't seen earlier)

  » The interviewers can revisit your profile and discover new information they may not have been aware of (eg honours, awards, recommendations etc)

  » The interviewers can see new posts that you make during the interview process (this builds recall and buy-in)

Keep exploring new roles

Finally, do not stop exploring new roles. I feel very strongly about this because so many people have one great interview and stop looking at other equally great opportunities. They then decline other roles and focus on the first one. It's important to note that the job interview process can take four to six weeks in total, and until you have an employment contract in hand, you have nothing.

Too many people come back to me regretting that they didn't pursue another role that would have been a great fit, because they were too focused on a job opportunity that looked like it was going to be offered to them. Let the potential employer stress about the fact that you are in discussions with other companies, and they might just move faster in offering you the job.

SWITCH TIP

Demand increases perceived value.

To close this chapter, I'd like to share the words of the vice president of a Fortune 100 company:

> 'Pree, when I want to make an offer to someone, I want to know that other companies in the industry are wanting them as well, because if not (and they are meant to be so good), I wonder, why am I the only one pursuing them?'

SWITCH ACTION

Having completed this chapter, write down at least one thing you've learned and one action you need to take. You may like to use the Switch actions sheet at www.switch.work/bonus to record your learning points and action plan.

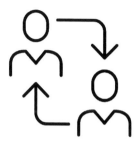

FOURTEEN

Negotiate To Reach Agreement

PRINCIPLE

Switch from a stand-off to a stand-out negotiation.

I had an unusual encounter on the Great Wall of China, when I innocently enquired from a hawker about the cost of a silk scarf to take back home as a souvenir for my wife. The moment she told me the price, I knew it was a rip-off and didn't want it any more. As I walked away, she ran behind me, grabbing my jacket and reducing the price by 30%, then 50% and finally 70%.

I stopped to listen, but I had decided I didn't want it anymore. She wouldn't let me go and spread her arms out sideways to prevent me from walking past her. My colleague was helpless with laughter, recording this on video. Finally, I saw a gap between the hawker's hands and the wall, so I darted off. Still she ran after me, but I wasn't stopping this time.

To negotiate means different things to different people. One person might talk about it in relation to a hostage situation. Another might think about bargaining down the price of a handmade artefact on holiday.

SWITCH TIP

Negotiation follows a similar pattern to the overall consultative process, where you seek to understand needs and provide suggestions that are mutually valuable and beneficial to all people involved.

When you think about negotiation in relation to the interview process, the most important thing to remember is that it will be a natural, easy and comfortable conversation if you have these conditions in place:

- You are thoroughly **prepared** for the interview

- You have good **rapport** with the interviewer

- You truly understand the **needs** of the company

- You have discussed **solutions** to the interviewer's problems and how to achieve their goals

- You have resolved every **objection**

- You check and **confirm** you are both in alignment

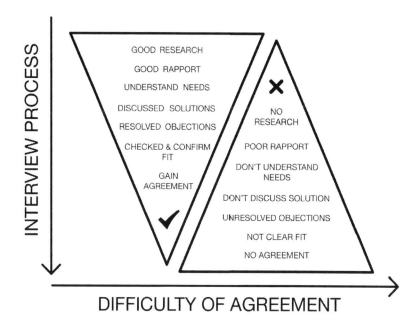

Stages of the interview and negotiation process

The triangle on the left shows what a good negotiation looks like. It is easy to reach agreement as every preceding stage has been done correctly, so the people involved both recognise the MVP and are being flexible.

The triangle on the right shows what a bad negotiation looks like. It is difficult to reach agreement because every preceding step in the interview process has not been done correctly, so the people involved don't value each other and are inflexible. This is how stand-offs are created during the negotiation stage, if you even get that far.

The more people recognise value, the more flexible they become.

Negotiate to get the right job

An interview process involves multiple stakeholders and their objectives, which are guided (and limited) by organisational policies, and more importantly, what you want from that job to make it right. Most people want:

- To be appreciated and supported

- To work in an organisation with a good culture

- To have work-life balance

- To have personal and professional growth

- To be well rewarded

Unfortunately, not every job scores 10/10 on each of these criteria. Some of these elements cannot be negotiated into a contract, for example appreciation and culture. They either already exist in the team and manager's behaviour, or they don't. And if they don't, don't accept that job. Keep looking.

But you can negotiate things like:

- Salary and benefits

- Working hours, days working from home, a cap on interstate or overseas travel

- Financial support for an MBA and time off to study for it (or any relevant professional development that will help you perform better at work and grow in your career)

Often the presence (or lack) of these factors will determine how much you enjoy your job, and how long you are likely to stay in it, so start with the end in mind and ensure you have negotiated the things that matter to you. The offer comparison tool will provide you with a clear comparison of your position, the company's position and the gaps between what you desire and what it is offering.

Using the offer comparison tool, available for download at www.switch.work/bonus, complete:

1. Priority scores. Write down a score from 1–7 for each of the job factors or areas listed on the table to help you determine your priorities. A score of 1 is your most important priority in your job and a score of 7 is the least critical. No two factors should have the same number.

2. Current situation. Write down points about the job you currently have (or may have had).

3. Job offer. Write down points about the job offer, which should have been provided early in the interview conversations with your primary point of contact (eg the hiring manager).

4. Desired situation. Write down points about what you want in the right job. Separate this information into three categories – good (minimum requirements), better (favourable requirements) and best (maximum requirements).

5. Assessment comparison. This represents the comparison between your current situation and your desired situation. Separate this information into three categories – more, same or worse – and then record by how much they differ (ie a percentage amount). Based on the allocation of your 1–3 priority scores, there should be an alignment with at least your desired minimum requirements (good). Going further, based on the allocation of your 4–7 priority scores, there should be an alignment with at least your current situation, unless you don't really care about scores 6 and 7. These are areas you could trade or remove from serious consideration.

6. Action points. This represents the action you will take. For every job factor that you have allocated a 1–3 priority score, you will need to ask for the minimum desired requirements (good) and be able to justify why you are worth it. Write down your justification points on the table which is available to download at www.switch.work/bonus.

The offer comparison tool

Factors	1. Priority scores	2. Current situation	3. Job offer	4. Desired situation	5. Assessment comparison	6. Action points
Salary						
Incentives/ bonuses/ commissions						
Benefits						
Travel						
Career development						
Workplace flexibility policies						
Anything else that matters to you (business values, purpose...)						

Once you've completed the recommended information on the offer comparison tool table, you should have a clear comparison of:

- Your position in relation to your minimum and maximum desired requirements

- The company's position and its job offer details

- The gaps (if any) between what you desire and the company's offer

Negotiate to influence and achieve alignment

Negotiations can involve a range of people, durations, agendas and variety based on the nature of the transaction. In the case of job offers, they are usually completed in a one-on-one manner over a few conversations. These are called integrative negotiations, where both parties are working towards a mutually beneficial outcome to arrive at the best possible agreement. This is in contrast to distributive negotiations, where each party is working towards getting as much as possible for themselves (eg the woman I encountered at the Great Wall of China).

In integrative negotiations, achieving alignment through identifying a range of mutually valuable outcomes is a powerful and influential factor. This enables people to come together, because they both want a similar or the same thing.

LISA'S STORY: ALIGNMENT IN NEGOTIATIONS

Lisa is a director of partnerships at a national company. She has spent five years in the role and built a thriving ecosystem of partners that generate new customers, but the company has announced a restructure and her job is expected to be phased out. She is actively exploring new jobs.

She meets Simon, the managing director of a smaller but fast-growing company. The company has a partnership program that has failed to deliver results – instead of contributing 33% of the revenue to the company, the partner program has yielded less than 5%. Simon feels that Lisa would be a good cultural fit. Her experience with partners is invaluable and her relationships would help the company grow this program rapidly.

Lisa is interested in the position. The only problem is that her current salary is $150,000 with an on-target earning potential of $250,000. The company has budgeted a salary of $120,000 with $200,000 on-target earnings potential. She believes this company culture and role are improvements on her current job and is financially comfortable, so she isn't needing an increase on her existing package and will accept a similar one.

Simon mentions that he is interested in extending an offer for her to work with the company, but is $30,000 short on base salary and $50,000 short on incentives. Lisa considers what he says and asks, 'What does an increase in partnership revenue from 5% to 33% equate to, based on your current estimates?'

Simon answers, '$3.3 million.'

Lisa then says, 'We both want a healthy partnership program and you can see that I know how to build one to where you would want it within twelve months. Would a total increase in revenues of $3.3 million be worth investing an extra $50,000 into my compensation plan? It's only 1.5% of the total amount.'

Simon sees her point and mentions that he would have to get approval from the board of directors, but agrees in principle that he will prepare an offer. Agreed. Done!

Lisa's story is an example of the benefits and process of achieving alignment through negotiation via these four steps:

1. Identifying what each person wants

2. Aligning what each person wants

3. Trading on what is not essential for each other

4. Agreeing and acting on next steps

Negotiate to unite people with a common goal

Negotiating to achieve mutually valuable outcomes draws people out of their own positions and unites them with a common goal. Building rapport and finding this common goal develops and maintains trust, and enables each party to influence and persuade the other/s. It reduces the resistance to change because it focuses people on the mutual value they will receive. And when there is focus on value, the resistance to price always goes down. Driving towards consensus builds trust and respect between both parties because this is just the beginning of a work relationship. There is so much more to come.

Negotiation follows a similar pattern to the overall consultative process, where you seek to understand needs and provide suggestions that are mutually valuable. Using real data in simple form can be effective to demonstrate the value of an investment and frame the whole conversation with a focus on the common good. This is always more successful than a hard-sell or an inflexible stand-off and brings people together to achieve a win-win situation.

SWITCH ACTION

Having completed this chapter, write down at least one thing you've learned and one action you need to take. You may like to use the Switch actions sheet at www.switch.work/bonus to record your learning points and action plan.

The Switch Method

Afterword:
Get Ready To Switch

Now that you have journeyed through this book, learning the history and the four steps of The Switch Method, it's time to implement this model to take you from your current situation to your desired future. You can stand out, be preferred and land the right job.

James was in his dream job as the managing director of a company in which he'd worked his way up through sales into sales leadership. But after five years, the company had to shut down due to financial problems. Devastated about the loss and the difficulty of finding a new leadership role – he had a family to support – James accepted a senior sales role.

I called him a number of times with opportunities to move to similar roles, but he was completely focused on moving into a leadership position within this company. After two and a half years of record-breaking results and having earned the respect and support of his team, he stepped into the country manager role. He had focused on the right fit and had found it within this organisation.

Sam had toyed with the idea of starting his own blog, but ended up writing an article on LinkedIn. He had a number of likes and positive comments from his network and someone even messaged him. As he had not connected with many of these people for a while, it felt good to be seen and heard, so he wrote some more and started commenting on other posts, sharing news about his own team and company and becoming more prominent in his network.

One day, because someone had read his article, they offered him a full expenses-paid trip to speak at an industry conference in Dubai. He went and presented at the event. After his talk, he was approached by a senior executive within the industry and invited to an exploratory conversation about a career with their company. He pursued it, liked it and was able to negotiate a great salary and benefits package, in addition to interesting work and other terms. He switched to being socially prominent and built a personal brand which helped him secure his next role.

Jenny was brought in by a global organisation as a sales manager to build a promising division. Twelve months into the job, and after consistent restructuring and changes, the person who'd brought her into the company had gone, along with other key people. In their place were people who were not a good cultural fit and she knew things wouldn't be great for too long.

She decided six months into the changes to start talking to companies that would value her experience. She made a list of targeted companies and contacts, and emailed, called and messaged them via LinkedIn. This resulted in seven self-sourced opportunities. And after a six-week interview process, she was able to negotiate the best terms for a new role because she had multiple opportunities and employers who really wanted her. She took ownership of her circumstances and proactively targeted employers she knew would recognise and value her industry experience.

Andrew, the sales director at a fast-growing pre-initial public offering company, met with Colin, an account executive, for an interview and immediately built common ground on the fact that both of them had previously worked in other parts of the world. Colin spent the initial part of the conversation asking Andrew questions about his problems, challenges and the results he wanted to achieve in the coming year. Andrew opened up early in the conversation and told him what they were. Colin then matched his experience and the results he'd had with the problems Andrew was facing.

At some point, the conversation changed from being an interview to a consultation. Colin was now the doctor and Andrew was the patient. As a result of Colin matching his experience to Andrew's problems, they easily transitioned into discussing what he would do once in the role. He developed influence, and the result was that Andrew offered him the position.

In each of these stories, a combination of focusing on the right fit, an impressive personal brand, relevant job targets and influence at interviews resulted in professionals successfully landing their jobs. This is what makes The Switch Method powerful and effective.

What's unique about The Switch Method are the multiple hours of working with professionals that underpin it, the tools and solutions I've developed that have brought results. It is a step-by-step method, supported by essential factors for success, and no individual step is greater than the whole. You need to understand, embrace and act upon it to completion so that you can have multiple job opportunities to consider. The Switch Method provides you with a roadmap to follow to achieve your goal faster without distractions, diversions and delays. You will know what to do at every step and avoid the pain of going three steps forward, then two steps back with every contradicting bit of advice.

The most effective thing you can do is act. If you are busy with work and home pressures, I recommend working through The Switch Method over a ninety-day period. If you are in between jobs, I recommend working through this in a fourteen-day period.

SWITCH TIP

You cannot control the outcome, but you can control the actions that lead to the outcome.

Start implementing The Switch Method today using the tools outlined in this book and access the templates at www.switch.work/bonus. I could add hundreds of stories to those of James, Sam, Jenny and Andrew, but the most important story is yet to be told: yours.

When you secure the right job for your next career move, please send me an email to ifoundit@switch. work. Your story could inspire thousands of people, just like James, Sam, Jenny and Andrew's stories might have inspired you. Now it's time to switch.

If you have received a few good ideas from this book to help you get the right job and build a great career, then my year-long journey – weekends at the office, writing during holidays and time away from my family – has been worth it. For additional help with implementation, visit me at www.switch.work.

References

Cobalt Community Research, 'Managing Community Engagement', not dated, HYPERLINK "http://www.cobalt-communityresearch.org/managing-employeeengagement. html" www.cobaltcommunityresearch.org/managing-employeeengagement.html [accessed 16 Jan 2020]

Maslow, Abraham, 'A Theory of Human Motivation', Psychological Review, 50(4), 1943, pp370-96

United Nations, 'Sustainable Development Goals', not dated, HYPERLINK "http://www.un.org/sustainabledevelopment/sustainable-development-goals/" www.un.org/sustainabledevelopment/sustainable-development-goals/ [accessed 16 Jan 2020]

Wigert B and Agrawal S, 'Employee Burnout, Part 1: The 5 Main Causes', Gallup, U.S.A., 12 July 2018, HYPERLINK "https://www.gallup.com/workplace/237059/employee-burnout-part-main-causes.aspx" www.gallup.com/workplace/237059/employee-burnout-part-main-causes.aspx [accessed 16 Jan 2020]

Wikipedia contributors, 'Albert Mehrabian', Wikipedia, The Free Encyclopedia, 4 September 2019, https://en.wikipedia.org/wiki/Albert_Mehrabian [accessed 16 Jan 2020]

Acknowledgements

The Switch Method is a result of thousands of life lessons I've learned from many mid- to senior-level managers and executives over the last ten years. I owe this book to these professionals and their willingness to be transparent, vulnerable and ask for help. Their courage and resilience are inspirational to me and I thank them for sharing their stories.

I value the input from each person who reviewed the book and provided me with feedback for improvement and praise that is at the front of this book.

I also am grateful for my team, Tia, Lynette, Sabine and Belinda, who have patiently reviewed and commented on revision after revision of the book.

I am grateful to my parents who have always encouraged me to go as far as I can and celebrated each step forward. But above all, I owe everything to the one true Author and Finisher; the Beginning and the End; the pulse in my veins, the breath in my lungs and the Source of every good idea and intention that has brought this book to life.

The Author

Pree Sarkar is an executive recruiter and career advisor to global technology companies and their mid to senior managers and professionals. He is the founder and chief advisor at Switch Talent and Career Accelerator.

Over the last twenty years, Pree has worked for and with Fortune 100 companies in sales, management and consulting roles. He spent his first ten years in a corporate career-focused role, rapidly rising to be the country sales director for FedEx Office by the age of thirty-two, leading a team of twenty-three which included sales managers, account executives and customer-service staff. He was an integral part of the senior leadership team, working closely with the managing director, HR, operations and finance.

Having experienced first-hand the problems and pain associated with management dysfunction, workplace problems and bad hiring, Pree moved into recruitment to help managers and employees find the right match and mutual value in their working relationships. As an executive recruiter, he has consulted to managing directors, vice presidents and sales directors at a number of global companies, as well as marketing, HR, customer service, IT, operations managers and executives.

Pree is the only non-US based member of the prestigious Pinnacle Society, the premier consortium of industry leading recruiters in North America, which helps him and his clients stay at the cutting edge of information and development across the recruitment and executive search profession. He is a certified and registered master practitioner in neuro-linguistic programming, which enables him to help people identify, resolve and overcome emotional barriers to performance. He has a university degree, a Post Graduate Diploma in Management, and certification in workplace training and assessment, as well as being a certified predictive index analyst for behavioural performance in the workplace. A top-performing recruiter for ten+ years now, he has placed hundreds of people and interviewed and coached thousands. LinkedIn rates Pree as the Top 1% recruiter.

Connect with Pree at:

⊡ linkedin.com/in/preesarkar
✉ pree@switch.work

Printed in Great Britain
by Amazon

57340093R00160